THE WHEEL OF
SUSTAINABILITY

Engaging and Empowering Teams
to Produce Lasting Results

ADAM LAWRENCE

THE WHEEL OF SUSTAINABILITY
© 2021 by Adam Lawrence
First Edition

Edited by Tessa Shaffer & Wendy Bolton
Cover design by Keith Bell
Interior design by Todd Keisling | Dullington Design Co.

THE WHEEL OF SUSTAINABILITY

Engaging and Empowering Teams to Produce Lasting Results

This book is dedicated to:

Peggy – My wife. She stood by me while I was writing, looked over every word, and made sure I told my stories in a meaningful way. We've been on quite a journey together, had many adventures, laughed a lot, cried a bit, and strengthened our relationship every day.

Tyler – My son and IT department. He has kept me out of trouble many times and figured out how to set things back to normal. You have grown to be a fine young man and I am very proud of you.

TABLE OF CONTENTS

PREFACE

PREFACE

People are the key to improvement.

We all have a story to tell. Mine is the story of the system I developed to help businesses sustain critical improvement efforts. I cranked up some tunes and started typing. Eventually, I arrived at the book you have in your hands.

I've always been intellectually curious and scientifically minded. That led me to complete an Industrial Engineering degree at Virginia Tech and then apply my background in industry. For more than thirty years, I've had the honor and privilege of helping teams all over the world solve complex problems, first in a corporate career and now as a consultant.

I think of myself as a *"Kaizen Ninja."* I help teams achieve their solutions in a way that seems like I'm not there. When necessary, I jump out of the background to provide a *gentle* nudge. Sometimes it feels more like a kick. Either way, it's all about helping teams own their results and win.

Nothing can stop people when they're engaged and empowered to use their creativity and work on things that are important to them. When teams I facilitated solved critical business problems and achieved breakthrough results, they expressed joy and relief. It was contagious.

As time went by, some of their results deteriorated and the original issues resurfaced. It bothered me that their hard work wasn't sustained. I was determined to do something about it. I shared my observations and concerns with others and did research. I felt compelled to learn how to sustainably solve problems.

I read voraciously and visited many businesses. The concept of sustainability seemed simple enough, but wasn't easily applied. I decided I should create a system to guarantee lasting results.

I framed my objective in this way:

"Develop a system to ensure results achieved by teams will be sustained in such a way that problems they solve don't resurface."

Over the years, I developed my system. I tested it in hundreds of situations and it held up. Whether it was in manufacturing, services, or transactional processes, it applied. At a conference, I shared my findings with other continuous improvement practitioners and leaders. During a lunch break, I drew an image of my system on a sheet of paper. To my surprise, many at the table copied my drawing on whatever they had with them, including napkins. I realized I had something that could help others.

Once I knew my system worked, I documented and shared it with others. I helped teams implement it. And I noticed something. People took notes. They posted illustrations of it on their office walls. Some used it to help teams they were leading and facilitating. Teams were now solving problems and they were staying solved.

The time has arrived to share my system with you. I call it the Wheel of Sustainability.

INTRODUCTION

INTRODUCTION

We solve problems every day. We want our solutions to stick, so the problems don't come back. Sometimes, even with the best efforts and intentions, the same problems resurface. There must be a better way to sustain the results you work so hard to achieve.

The Wheel of Sustainability is the better way.

The Wheel provides a framework that's easy to follow and implement. But don't let the simple nature fool you. The Wheel of Sustainability is a system. Its strength lies in its eight spokes working in concert. The central hub of the Wheel holds everything together.

In this book, I'll explain all elements of the Wheel of Sustainability – what they mean, how they work, how to develop and implement them, and how to build the Leadership Commitment to implement the Wheel. With examples and stories of teams who used the Wheel to sustain their critical results, you'll learn about these and other inspiring efforts:

1. A team in Pennsylvania reduced late delivery fines received from Amazon from $1.2 million annually to $0 in three days. Those fines haven't returned. (Chapter 10)
2. A team in Washington cut their changeover time in half and are maintaining the best operating results in their history. (Chapter 3)
3. How painting tools *"pink"* kept them from being lost ever again in a factory in Ohio. (Chapter 4)

Even though the Wheel of Sustainability was developed using proven Lean principles, you don't have to be a Lean expert to use it. Don't fret. I'll provide enough background to help you understand the thinking behind the Wheel and why it works.

By the time you finish reading this book, you should be confident in your abilities to implement the Wheel of Sustainability for any project, team effort, or problem you intend to solve. You don't have to wait for a new problem to surface. You can apply the Wheel to work you're doing right now. Here's how I'm going to help you get there.

Following an overview, each successive chapter covers an individual element of the Wheel of Sustainability. Within each chapter, you'll find sections dedicated to:

- An introductory overview
- Principles
- Stories of successful use
- A story with less than successful results
- An example in the home or office
- Design and implementation tips
- Mistakes to avoid
- How Leadership Commitment supports successful implementation
- Summary
- Key takeaways note page

All stories in the book are true. Team member names have been changed. Company names are not stated.

I recommend reading the chapters in order. Elements of the Wheel build on each other and work together. You're welcome to skip around to get reinforcing information around the elements of the Wheel you're less familiar with. It's possible you may lose a bit of context or a reference from a prior chapter. Please don't skip the chapter on Leadership Commitment. It ties all of the elements together and provides an image of what's required for overall system success.

Some of the terms I use are from my perspective and may not match your definitions. I'll explain my thinking and you can decide whether you agree or not. I welcome any feedback you may have. If you want to know more about the Wheel, learn how to apply it in your situation, or just want to chat, contact me anytime:

Email – atlawrence@pi-partners.com
Cell – +1 (717) 947-5535
Website – www.pi-partners.com
LinkedIn Company Page – Process Improvement Partners
LinkedIn Personal Page – Adam Lawrence
YouTube Channel – Adam Lawrence

There's so much more I want to tell you about the Wheel of Sustainability. You don't have to *reinvent the wheel* in order to achieve and sustain amazing results. You just have to start spoke by spoke.

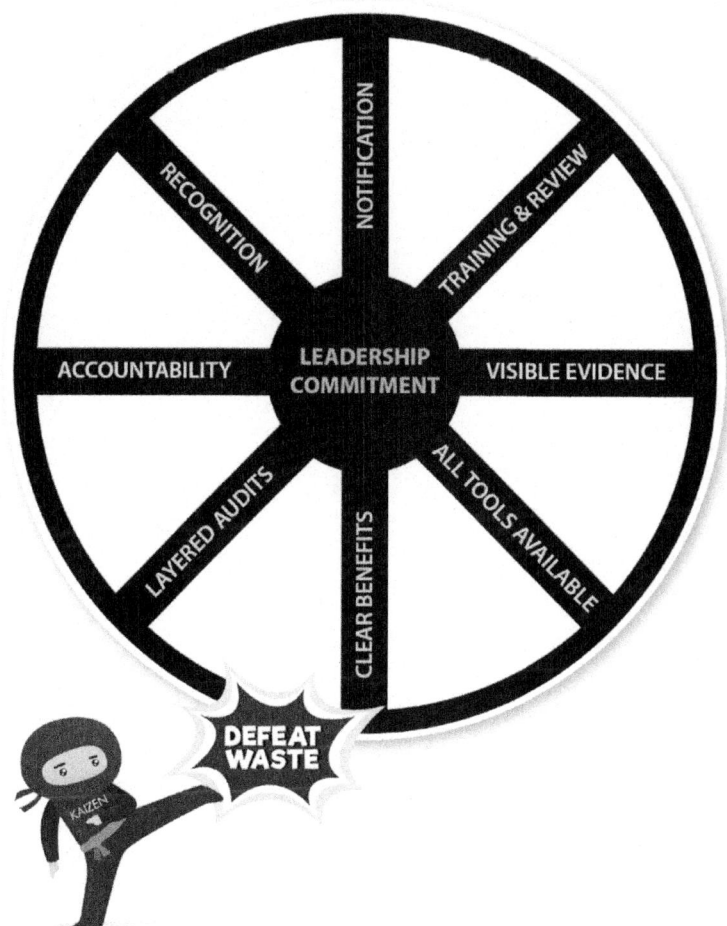

EIGHT SPOKES AND A HUB
AN OVERVIEW OF THE WHEEL OF SUSTAINABILITY

The Wheel of Sustainability is a system.

This chapter provides an overview of the Wheel of Sustainability. Successive chapters describe each component of the Wheel in greater detail.

The use of the Wheel relies on individuals, teams, or the organization's desire to drive improvement and then sustain the changes that have been designed, planned, and/or implemented.

There are eight spokes and one central hub. The Wheel requires all elements to be applied to the changes. Like any wheel, removing a spoke reduces its strength. Without the hub, the Wheel falls apart. Follow the Wheel clockwise, starting at 12 o'clock:

Notification – Changes to a process or procedure are communicated to the organization. People get the opportunity to hear about the changes, ask questions, and observe organizational commitment around them.

Training and Review – Those affected by the changes are trained using the structure of tell, show, and do. The trainer tells the learner what to do. Next, the trainer demonstrates how to do it. Finally, the learner demonstrates their ability to do it the way the trainer has presented.

Visible Evidence – The proper way to follow the changes is made visible. The visualization makes it almost impossible to do the wrong thing. Status is easily determined from a distance.

All Tools Available – Everything necessary to accomplish the changes safely and productively is provided, logically arranged, and in close proximity. If there are multiple locations in need of the same tools, they are duplicated and placed in each location. Tools can be physical or virtual.

Clear Benefits – Those following the changes must see them as simpler, more logical, less stressful, and safer to accomplish, in order to fully adopt them.

Layered Audits – Leaders audit and engage with those doing the work associated with the changes to ensure it is understood and accomplished properly. If there are any deviations, auditors provide help and support to return to standard.

Accountability – When someone is not properly doing the work associated with the changes, leaders must engage to understand why and provide immediate help and/or more training.

Recognition – Sharing stories of success helps people make the connection to improved results due to the changes, locking in their commitment.

The hub of Leadership Commitment connects the spokes of the Wheel of Sustainability:

Leadership Commitment – Leaders visibly commit to help, support, audit, and provide everything necessary to make the work of the team successful. They understand how the changes impact overall performance and demonstrate commitment to the changes. They do everything possible to ensure their teams win.

There is overlap and synergy among the elements of the Wheel. They should all be considered together as a system. Omitting a spoke will reduce the strength of the Wheel. If there isn't true Leadership Commitment to implementing the Wheel and all spokes, the system falls apart.

When I introduce the Wheel of Sustainability to a team, I challenge them to implement and test all elements of the Wheel for the improvements and changes they develop. How will they notify people, train them, provide Visible Evidence, and consider all other elements?

One of the critical tests is to approach people unfamiliar with the proposed changes and gather their feedback. The less filtered the feedback, the better. People generally think negatively about changes, so team members are challenged to review with people *one on one*. Team members split up and find others to engage in discussion. In this way, they can genuinely listen to people's feedback and concerns. This avoids groupthink or mob mentality, where people's negative reactions may spin out of control and individual concerns may not be heard.

If a team is developing changes to be implemented by the greater organization, they must have authorization, support, and commitment from management and/or leadership. The team is walking a fine line. They aren't always the authority and can't hold people personally accountable to follow the changes. They must be empowered to drive the changes. Leadership Commitment empowers them.

Before diving into the Wheel of Sustainability in greater detail, I want to define some terms I am going to use in subsequent chapters.

Lean – A continuous improvement methodology, modeled after the Toyota Production System. Lean is focused on the customer and the relentless elimination of non-value-added activities (*waste*).

Waste – Anything the customer is unwilling to pay for, but occurs in a process. These are the non-value-adding steps. There are eight wastes:

Transportation, Inventory, Motion, Waiting, Overproduction, Over Processing, Defects, and Unused Employee Creativity.

Kaizen – A Japanese term meaning *"make something better"*. It can be a little or a lot better.

Kaizen Event – Bring people together for a set period of time to make improvements to a situation, process, or system. Event duration can be anywhere from hours to days.

5S – A workplace organization methodology used to improve the safety and productivity of a space or a system. The 5S's are: Sort, Set in Order, Shine, Standardize, and Sustain.

Standard Work – The best-known combination of people and machines to accomplish a task or perform a service, utilizing the minimum amount of labor, space, inventory, and equipment.

Gemba – A Japanese term, meaning *"the place where work is done. The real place. The real situation"*.

Gemba Walk – A tour of the workplace used to assess the health of the operating system. This can be a physical or virtual walk.

Value Stream – A series of processes creating the flow of value to the customer. Value can be delivered as a product or service.

Value Stream Mapping – A strategic planning approach that views value creation from the eyes of the customer. Anything that does not create value is identified as *waste* and plans are developed to reduce or eliminate the largest sources of *waste*.

Facilitator – Guides a team through a process, in order to arrive at a solution to a problem.

Sponsor – Identifies a problem to be solved, has authority to provide resources, and engages the facilitator to help the team.

Charter – A contract between the sponsor, facilitator, team leader, and team to solve a critical business problem.

A Preview of Leadership Commitment

Before moving to the individual spokes of the Wheel of Sustainability, let's take a quick look at Leadership Commitment. It's what holds the Wheel together. Leadership must be committed from the very top of the organization in order for any transformation to be successful. This is easier said than done. It can be difficult for leaders to visualize what's required of them in support of their teams' efforts. The Wheel provides an image of what commitment looks like in order to sustain positive results.

Leaders will be expected to engage with every element of the Wheel of Sustainability in a supportive way. There will be times when they'll have to drop what they're doing in order to correct an unproductive behavior and provide help (Accountability). Leaders will be required to assess the health of the improved system at a defined frequency (Layered Audits).

At the outset, leaders participate in the communication of changes to the organization (Notification) and engage in deeper conversations around the *how* and *why* of the change (Training and Review). When employees question how changes will help them personally (Clear Benefits), leaders share success stories demonstrating cause and effect (Recognition). Leaders look for signs that things are working as expected (Visible Evidence) and supply everything necessary to support the changes (All Tools Available).

During my initial discussions with organizational leaders, I describe the Wheel of Sustainability and what's expected of *them* as teams use it to implement improvements and changes. This is the first test of Leadership Commitment. If they flinch or appear uncomfortable with the amount of effort to be expended in support of their team, it's a strong indication of the challenges we'll face. If leaders are open and supportive, the team has a great chance to win.

When I gauge leaders' initial interest in the Wheel of Sustainability, my hope is they'll be curious enough to ask questions and express their commitment to it. For most, the Wheel is a new concept. The desire to sustain team efforts is not.

In the following chapters of this book, I share stories about projects and events I facilitated. You may be wondering what led to their inception. Working with my sponsor(s), we used a chartering process. Although I will describe it in greater detail in the chapter on Leadership Commitment (Chapter 10), it's important enough to provide context.

Chartering is a contract between the sponsor(s), facilitator, team leader, and the team. The sponsor authorizes the team to solve a problem the business has been struggling with using their current approach. The facilitator is engaged to help the team reach their solution. Chartering answers these key questions:

1. **Problem statement** – What is the problem to be solved? Why is it important to solve it? What's the impact to the customer, employees, organization, and/or shareholders? What is the compelling reason to solve it? Is there safety, financial, customer service, or other measures that would be positively impacted by solving the problem? What is the scope of the problem to be solved? Where does it start and where does it end?
2. **Objectives** – If the problem were solved, what would the evidence look like? Have we impacted time, cost, safety risk, or another key metric in a positive way? How would the team know they have won? What would constitute a breakthrough? Can it be seen?
3. **The team** – Who will help us solve the problem? Do they care about the problem enough to dedicate themselves to the effort? Are they personally impacted by or frustrated by the problem? Do the team members want to win?

4.   **Owner of the output** – When the effort is complete, who has the responsibility for the output of the team? Who will assure that the team does its work in the best interest of the organization? Once defined, this must be the team leader.

Once the charter is established and leadership displays their commitment, we build a plan for the work to engage and empower teams to solve complex problems. The Wheel of Sustainability is woven into that plan. Leaders gain a deeper understanding of the expectations for their role during the implementation of the Wheel during the project or event.

Chapter 10 will go into more detail and provide examples of Leadership Commitment. For now, consider how Leadership Commitment applies as you learn about each element of the Wheel. At the end of each chapter is a series of questions for you to consider to reinforce understanding and expectations for Leadership Commitment.

Now it's time to dig deeper into the Wheel of Sustainability. Ready? Let's go!

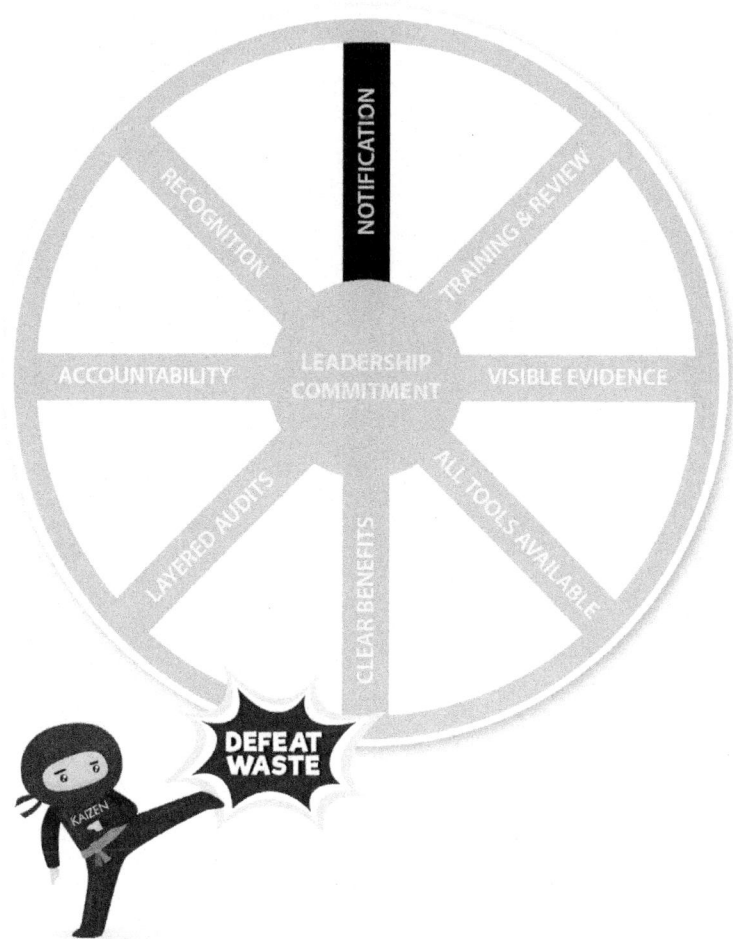

CHAPTER 2

NOTIFICATION

Notification is the act of communicating changes to the organization in a way that secures their commitment.

Introduction

Notification is the critical first step to sustainment. How the organization is notified of critical changes matters. The aim is to create awareness, alignment, and commitment to follow the new standard. Notification comes in many forms: crew meetings, town halls, one on ones, emails, department meetings, video conferences, and others. It could be argued any of these methods can be meaningful and successful. Some are more impactful than others. Let's explore some of these methods and the challenges they present.

Large meetings, with many in the audience

It's difficult to present information in a way that's engaging and allows people the time and comfort to ask questions and be heard. It's easy to be distracted. The presenter can't tailor the message to the needs of

31

everyone in the audience. The message may be diluted to the lowest common denominator. If people in the back of the room can't hear the speaker, they'll tune out. If someone wants to answer an email on their mobile device, who's going to stop them?

Video conference calls

People may multitask and work on other things unrelated to the topic being reviewed. They can be easily distracted by activities going on around them. If they turn off their camera or put themselves on mute, there's no way to know if they're paying attention.

One-on-one discussions

When speaking with someone one-on-one, they can't hide their feelings or be easily distracted. Although it requires a greater investment of time and effort to use this approach, I recommend it for critical transfer of information.

Adult learners retain around 10 percent of what they hear. If the message isn't compelling, don't expect that much. How do you make the message compelling? It must resonate with you first. If it doesn't, there's no way you can make it meaningful to others.

> We retain approximately 10 percent of what we see; 30 to 40 percent of what we see and hear; and 90 percent of what we see, hear, and do. We all have the capability to learn via all three styles, but are usually dominant in one.[1]

When I was growing up, my mother expected me to make my bed and keep my room clean and organized. She notified me of this requirement with great passion. "If you live in my house, you'll follow my rules." I didn't find her words compelling. One day, I learned a lesson the hard way. My homework was *accidently* thrown out with the other garbage in my room. I had to redo the work and stay up way past my normal bedtime. I worked under duress and missed important play and

---

[1] Principles of Adult Learning & Instructional Systems Design - NHI INSTRUCTOR DEVEL OPMENT COURSE
https://www.nhi.fhwa.dot.gov/downloads/freebies/172/pr%20pre-course%20reading%20assignment.p

sleep time. I won't say I regularly made my bed and cleaned my room from then on, but I did put my homework in a place where it couldn't be confused with the garbage.

Notification in its most effective form is delivered by leaders who believe in the change they're reviewing. Examples include:

- It's the right thing to do.
- People will be better off.
- A critical problem has been solved.
- Direct involvement in making the changes.

People will observe the speaker to check for alignment with the information delivered. They're not easily fooled. Transparency and truthfulness are the best approach.

Notification in its least effective form comes when the leader doesn't care about or believe in the change being communicated. They may say, "this is the new policy, they're making us implement it," or "this is the change, you have to do it." Those affected by the change may be unwilling to comply. If it's not good enough for leaders, why should it be good enough for them?

Human nature is to react negatively to changes, especially when they're not well explained. People expect the worst, and hope for the best. If you help them see the change as a good thing, they will fight the urge to take a negative view of it.

Principles of Notification

- Leaders participate in Notification to demonstrate their commitment.
- Those delivering the Notification know the *why* as well as the *what* of changes being implemented.
- Notification is delivered to the audience in an engaging and non-distracting way.
- The message is compelling to the speaker and audience.

Success Stories

Beer Is the Answer

Early in my career, I was offered a position as a shift supervisor at a ceiling grid plant near Chicago. I received supervisor training the prior year. This was my first opportunity to use what I learned in the "real world". From my second-floor office, I could see both ends of the plant, which included eleven operating lines, offices, and a warehouse. What immediately struck me was the lack of focus on the quality of the product we were producing.

In my first days on the job, I was extremely interested in helping make improvements to the process. It was challenging. I had no experience in the industry and the crew knew it. I had to find a way to connect with my crew and build trust. It turns out beer was the way to make this connection – but not in the way you might think.

Ceiling grid is made from coil steel, which is roll-formed into shape and cut into bars of varying lengths. These bars are then fed into a punch press, which trims the bars to final length and cuts holes and forms end details on them. It seemed like more bars of grid were going into scrap bins than were being packed for shipment to our customers. This scrap material would be sent to a recycler, who paid pennies on the dollar for the precious bars. We were losing money. I was determined to stop our losses.

I met with my crew and discussed our high scrap rate. I noticed some heads were down. A few were muttering things under their breath. I overheard, "this new guy doesn't know what he's talking about." Some were more interested in what their neighbor was doing than what I was talking about. I decided to press the issue and was able to get one crew member to speak up. She said the process was to blame and there was little she could do about it.

As I talked about scrap as a percentage of the total grid produced, I noticed rolling eyes of disapproval. The crew seemed unimpressed with the number. One brave soul said he would try to reduce scrap as best he could. He was met with grunts and other sounds of objection.

A few weeks passed and our scrap performance wasn't getting any better. I met with my crew again. They told me they were doing their best, but didn't know what they could do to improve performance. Frustrated, I met with my Plant Manager to see if he had any ideas for me to use.

He told me the scrap rate was quite high during his time at the plant. In the years prior to his arrival, it had been significantly lower. What changed, I wondered? My next stop was to talk to one of our technical resources. Bob had been a supervisor in the plant for many years before I arrived.

Me: "I don't know what to do. I don't seem to be able to get the crew to care about our high scrap rate."

Bob: "I don't want to rub it in, but my crew cared more about quality when I was their supervisor."

Me: "You can't leave me hanging like that. What do you mean they cared more about quality?"

Bob: "We had stability in the plant for many years. People worked as a team and were focused on doing their best together. Now things are different."

Me: "What's changed?"

Bob: "There are a lot of new people managing the plant, including you. There are trust issues."

Me: "I'm a stand-up guy. Why don't you think they trust me?"

Bob: "The crew doesn't know you. You're young enough to be their son. Trust is built over time. They're not ready to follow you yet."

I knew I had to improve the situation and didn't have years to do it. I had to come up with something meaningful to make a connection with my crew. One day, while grocery shopping with my wife, I noticed the store sold beer along with food. This was something I hadn't seen growing up in Maryland. As I looked at the prices of the beer, I was inspired. I was now ready for my next crew meeting.

I told my crew I didn't have the experience or the knowledge to solve our scrap problem. But, through the inspiration of beer, I now knew how to help them. "You see," I began, "a two-foot bar of ceiling grid has the same value as a can of beer." They looked at me strangely and one crew member let a laugh slip out. "A four-foot bar of grid is worth two cans of beer, and a twelve-foot bar equals a six-pack. If we reduce the amount of grid in the scrap bins, we'd save enough money to have an open bar at the next company party."

It was as if a light turned on in the room. My message was compelling enough that the crew started asking questions and making observations about possible scrap causes. They shared scrap reduction ideas. There was energy and enthusiasm in their voices. They were on a mission to have a great company party.

Over the next few days, I reminded the crew how much beer was sitting in the scrap bins. Instead of percentages, we were now talking about something of value and meaning to them. I didn't realize how much it meant. One day, a mechanic came to my office and told me he had saved a keg of beer for the company on his last setup. He was able to get everything right on the first try. His scrap bin was almost empty.

Something else was happening. Crew members were talking with me as an equal. They were friendlier, more personable, and welcomed me into more discussions. Beer was usually the start to our conversations, but we quickly moved on to a wide range of other topics, such as sports, the weather, our families, and even work. Crew meetings became more engaging. Team members shared their thoughts and ideas freely. We became a team.

Over the next few months, our scrap rate came down dramatically, and settled to 75 percent below the historical average. Bob was amazed and even admitted that the scrap rate hadn't been so low when he was the supervisor. I told him he had inspired me to come up with something to get the crew's attention and make a connection. In a town like Chicago, beer was the answer.

Attention to Detail

I moved my family across country to become Production Manager for a ceiling tile plant in Oregon. The plant had a strong team-based culture. People helped each other work in as safe and productive a manner as possible. It wasn't unusual to see our Plant Manager on the factory floor, assisting the technicians with their work or coaching them around their safety behaviors.

However, plant performance had deteriorated over the years and we were operating at less than budgeted levels. I was determined to identify the reasons and work with the technicians to turn things around.

The first two months of my time at the plant, I spent more time on the factory floor than in meetings or in my office. I came into the plant any hour of the day or night, trying to assess and understand the reasons for the lowered performance. People had the right attitude. They wanted to win. What was holding them back?

The Team Managers had strong relationships with their crews. The equipment was in good condition and there was an established preventive maintenance program. Something was missing. I had to find out what it was.

One morning, while taking a walk around the plant, I noticed papers on clipboards at each operating station. They were titled "*While Running Tasks*". These were process checks to be completed and signed off by the technicians on shift. There were many blank spaces on the papers, meaning that checks weren't completed.

I reviewed all of the papers and determined less than half of the checks had been completed and signed off. Team Managers told me the checks were critical to the performance and safety of the line. Teams of technicians had identified and agreed to the tasks. They met every three months to review and update *While Running Tasks* as new issues arose.

I studied the forms to see if there was any correlation between tasks not completed and downtime or scrap events. In a two-month sample, more than one-third of the downtime and scrap events could have been prevented if the checks were completed properly and on time. I now knew what had to be done.

Aligning with the three Team Managers, we came up with a plan to rapidly improve performance. We would rededicate ourselves to the *While Running Tasks*. Nothing less than a 100 percent completion rate was acceptable. Technicians would be accountable to complete and sign off on all tasks during their shift. Team Managers would audit the tasks on every shift, and I'd audit randomly every day and do a full audit of all checklists at the end of every week.

We planned crew meetings to share the new requirements and expectations. All of us would participate in every meeting, demonstrating alignment, commitment, and belief in our new focus. The meetings were scheduled for the next day at 6:30 a.m., 3:30 p.m., and 10:30 p.m.

I kicked off each meeting by telling the crews how impressed I was by their teamwork and honesty. No one ever signed off on anything unless they had actually completed a task. Now, it was time to use those strengths to improve performance.

I shared examples of line failures and scrap events directly impacted by the incompletion of the critical *While Running Tasks* they had identified and agreed to. We owed it to each other to honor our commitments. Next, we laid out our principles and expectations:

1. **Attention to detail** will improve performance and keep everyone safe.
2. *While Running Tasks* are the first line of defense to prevent problems and reduce safety risk.
3. Anything less than 100 percent compliance to *While Running Tasks* increases risk for downtime, scrap, and injuries.
4. Completing *While Running Tasks* is a condition of employment.

Each Team Manager described how he'd work with his crew to attain 100 percent compliance. He'd hold himself and each crew member accountable to their *While Running Tasks*. Crews were encouraged to review the *While Running Tasks* and verify they were relevant and would prevent problems.

We fielded many questions. It was easy to answer any concerns. We truly believed this approach was going to keep everyone safer and more productive. People were worried they were going to be fired if they forgot a task. We understood and established levels of discipline. We didn't want to fire anyone. We did believe that 100 percent compliance was the best strategy to improve performance. We couldn't compromise our beliefs.

The first two weeks after the meetings, a few tasks were forgotten. Some discipline was recorded. No one was fired. Compliance reached 90 percent in the first month with renewed focus. Plant performance noticeably improved. The second month, we hit 98 percent. One hundred percent compliance was achieved in the third month. Everyone could tell the difference. The plant was running significantly better. For the next year and a half, we stayed at 100 percent. During that time, the plant attained company records for performance. Attention to detail cost us nothing, except time, focus, and commitment.

Less than Success Stories

Listen to Your People, People

Our Research and Development team identified the need to reduce the time it took from the identification of a new product idea to launch of the new product. Many believed *"you can't schedule invention."* Working with the Director, we chose to focus on the work leading up to and supporting the invention, even if we couldn't specify its timing. We agreed to use a three-day Value Stream Mapping (VSM) event to develop their strategic plan.

> **Value Stream Mapping**
>
> *A strategic planning approach that views the creation and delivery of value from the eyes of the customer. Anything that does not create value is identified as "waste" and plans are developed to reduce or eliminate the largest sources of waste.*

After reviewing Lean principles and aligning around the charter, we took a Gemba walk to observe the current state of the process. Those who haven't participated in a VSM don't appreciate how critical it is to understand the current state. They want to work on the future state, thinking they already know the issues, pain, and problems. The current state review is where "A-ha" moments occur. This leads to a stronger plan for the future state.

The team wondered how to walk their process. Much of their work happened on their computers, at their desks, in labs, and testing facilities. Ever the optimist, I encouraged the team to walk to where the work was done to uncover anything helpful on their journey to the future state. Although skeptical, they agreed to follow my lead. We walked around the offices first.

We observed people working at their desks. I asked questions about what they were doing. They did their best to explain things. Most team members weren't taking notes or asking follow-up questions.

The next stop was at a large wall containing a wide variety of graphs, charts, and documents. The R&D Director stopped us there. He proudly explained how he communicated with his people and how much they used the posted information. The team seemed satisfied with the explanation. It looked like a bunch of clutter to me. There was so much paper that it was unclear what was important, relevant, and critical to the work of the employees.

I walked over to Andy, a Scientist who was working at his desk, and invited him to join us.

Me: "What do you think of the information posted on the wall?"

Andy: "I don't know, I never look at it."

All team members, including the R&D Director, were shocked. Was Andy the only one who didn't use the information? Others working in the area confirmed they didn't use the information on the board either.

Not wanting to insult our leader, I asked team members to write their observations about the wall of information on their Post-it notes. We continued our Gemba walk, taking note of other issues as we saw them. Team members started engaging and asking tougher questions in their efforts to identify improvement opportunities.

After we completed our walk, the team listed all of the steps in the current process and the issues and problems they identified. One of the biggest problems was the lack of communication of relevant information to the scientists. It was just as our brave Scientist had said during the Gemba walk. With proper Notification, the scientists could have helped design the information in a way that would be helpful to them.

The team knew what it had to do: Provide visible, relevant, and timely information to the scientists in a way that would help them do their work every day. During the rest of the VSM, the team built a path to the future state that significantly reduced time from new product idea to launch.

Much of the effort centered around providing the proper information to the people who needed it. Instead of assuming what was needed, they included the scientists and technicians in the development of the communication solution. Examples included:

- Standard questions reviewed at the weekly huddle for every key project.
- Red/green status indicators for every project to identify when help was needed.
- Bi-weekly visual review of the status of all projects, held at the information wall. Each project owner was responsible for describing progress and issues keeping the project from moving forward.
- Increased participation and engagement in the weekly lab and testing facility Gemba walk.

Over time, the communication plan was refined. The team created feedback loops to verify the communication was helping employees do their work. Ultimately, the time from new product idea to launch was reduced from eighteen to ten months. More importantly, the team realized how important it is to include people in the design of systems used for their benefit. One properly posed question can save months of effort.

Never Give Up – How We Almost Lost Our Team Members

A toothpaste manufacturer requested my help for the first Kaizen event in the history of its New Jersey factory. During the site assessment, we identified many candidates for improvement. Plant leadership prioritized the first area to work on.

Aligning with the Continuous Improvement Manager, Plant Manager, and corporate support, we chartered a Kaizen event focused on improving the performance of the materials preparation area. Positive results would be visible and  build momentum for the Lean transformation at the plant.

During the chartering process, my sponsor answered these questions to uncover the value and opportunity of the Kaizen event:

1. What's the problem you want to solve? What's the value of solving it for the customer, the employees, and the company?
2. What are the measurable objectives of the Kaizen event? What does a win look like?
3. Who are the team members invested in the problem enough to help you solve it? Who can help us win?
4. Who owns the output when the Kaizen event is over?

Using the answers to the charter questions, the Kaizen event was designed to create a win for the plant. Because it was their first event, we had to take into account little to no continuous improvement experience on the team.

The leadership team was advised to communicate as much as possible to the plant and the team in advance of the Kaizen event. This included talking with each team member individually to gain their alignment and commitment to the effort. Although they thought it was an extreme approach, they assured me they would follow my advice. Demonstrating his commitment, the Operations Manager took the role of Team Leader. If only they had used the principles of Notification, there would have been fewer misunderstandings.

Thirteen team members assembled in a meeting room and were trained in Lean principles on the morning of the first day of the Kaizen. Afterwards, we took a Gemba walk to assess the *current state* and identify opportunities to improve safety and performance. Each team member took Post-it notes and pens with them and were instructed to write down ideas for review after the tour.

We spent more than two hours in the factory. Team members were writing feverishly. They were seeing things in a new way and uncovering many issues associated with the process. As facilitator, I was pleased to see them identifying things as *waste* they had put up with in their normal jobs.

When we returned to the meeting room, everyone except one team member had written ideas on their Post-its. While this isn't unheard of, it's a signal something is wrong and needs to be dealt with. In total, the team had written more than 130 ideas for review and prioritization. This story isn't about those ideas, it's about team members who weren't properly prepared with strong Notification and had a challenging Kaizen event experience.

The Story of Chuck

Chuck didn't write down any ideas while the team was on the Gemba walk. When we returned to the meeting room, the team shared their ideas one at a time. The ideas were posted on a flip chart. I asked Chuck to write any ideas that might come to mind while others were sharing theirs.

He still didn't write anything. Looking for other ways for him to contribute, he was asked to post the flip charts of ideas on the wall as they were filled. Chuck seemed content and appeared to be listening to everyone's ideas.

After all ideas were shared, the team prioritized them. With five votes each, everyone picked the top ideas they thought would provide the greatest benefit. Chuck voted and the top three priority projects were identified. Each team member then picked the project they personally wanted to work on.

Chuck put his name on the project called *"organize the materials batching and testing area"*. Following this, the team was broken into sub-teams of four or five members. The sub-teams started to work on and conceptualize their solution before the end of the first day. Everything seemed okay with Chuck at this point.

The next morning, Chuck wasn't in the meeting room when the team reconvened. No one knew where he was. They thought he might be in the plant. Once the sub-teams started working on their projects, I went looking for him.

Chuck had gone back to his normal job in the materials receiving area. He thought it was more important than the Kaizen event. I explained his input was critical and convinced him to rejoin the team.

Once there, he worked with the team for the rest of the week. He was unfamiliar with the area the team was working in and didn't realize his input and perspective were important and valued. No one had explained the significance of this effort to him prior to the Kaizen.

The Story of Ethan

Ethan was a Mechanical Supervisor. He was picked for the team based on his extensive knowledge, team focus, and ability to get things done in short order. He seemed like a perfect team member for the first Kaizen event. Apparently, nobody had explained this to him.

Ethan shared many improvement ideas on the first day of the Kaizen. When the team prioritized their work, he seemed unhappy with one of the highest priority projects. This project was focused on improving air flow in the work space and received votes from five of the team members.

Although it wasn't directly associated with the charter objectives, it generated interest from the production operators. They said it impacted their productivity, safety, and the ability to get their work done in an error-free way, which *was* one of the charter objectives. They formed a sub-team to work on it.

At the end of the day, the sub-team couldn't solve the air-flow problem themselves and needed help from Ethan. They asked him to assess the air-handling unit. Ethan didn't agree it was worth his time. When pushed by the team, Hal grudgingly got up from his seat and said he would have the system checked before the next day.

The next morning, I asked the team to reflect on the first day of the first Kaizen event in the plant's history. When it was Ethan's turn, he said he had nothing to say and everything was okay. It was obvious he didn't feel that way. When pushed to say more, he put two thumbs up.

That's not what the team needed to hear. Pushed a bit more, the floodgates opened. Ethan told team members he thought they were working on the wrong things and he didn't sign up for this event. He was *"volun-told"* to attend. He thought the team should be working on things they could control and not finger-pointing at mechanical issues. After he said his piece, we thanked him for speaking up and helping us refocus on the things we could control and improve during the week.

As the week wore on, Ethan was visibly happier and more engaged. By the end of the week, he was extremely proud of all the work the team was able to accomplish. The air-handling unit was repaired and air flow was noticeably improved. Ethan even mentioned he was happy he had decided to speak up at the beginning of day two to get everyone back on track.

The Story of James

James's story was the most surprising to me. He seemed aligned with the efforts of the team throughout the week. On the morning of the third day, he arrived ten minutes before kickoff and told the Team Leader he didn't want to be on the team anymore.

He felt he hadn't been communicated with properly prior to the event, was forced to attend, and didn't agree with the team's focus. Although he had been relatively quiet earlier in the week, he was participating and contributing ideas up until this revelation. He told us we weren't listening to his issues and were working on the wrong things. We tried to reason with him and described how the team makes decisions in a Kaizen event. He was steadfast in his objections.

Then he said, "*I don't want to be here.*" We knew we shouldn't press the issue any longer. We thanked him for his contributions, told him we were sorry to see him go and hoped the efforts of the team would benefit him in his job at the plant. At that, he left to go back to his normal job.

It was time to have a discussion with Sue, the Plant Manager. We needed to understand how things ended up this way. She was shocked to hear the reasons team members wanted to quit the team. Sue thought we were heading in the right direction and was concerned we might not make the expected Kaizen breakthroughs if we lost any team members.

Sue was surprised about James and wanted to convince him to return. Although I wasn't sure this was a good idea, she was the Plant Manager and had every right to try. An hour later, James returned and reconnected with the team. We welcomed him back with kind words and handshakes.

The Team Leader took James and other team members down to the factory floor and let them show him their issues. He committed to write work orders for any issues that couldn't be resolved during the week.

James was pleased his voice was being heard. Many work orders were written, and some work had already been completed, much to his satisfaction. The rest of the team appreciated the quick resolution of the work orders.

By the fourth and final day, James was complimenting all of us for our support. Although he didn't present at the end of the Kaizen event, he shared positive feedback to all who asked him about his experience.

After the presentation ended, plant leadership held a wrap-up meeting with me. We covered many topics, most notably the things we could do to improve the experience for the next Kaizen team members. Now that the plant had Kaizen event experience, they could explain what to expect during the week. They vowed to be more visible in their preparations, use the principles of Notification, and hold individual conversations with potential team members.

This Kaizen was one of the more exhausting ones for me. With focus on the engagement and mood of the team, the effort felt much greater than usual. Had we lost these team members, there would have been many negative repercussions:

- Fewer resources to help accomplish our objectives.
- The loss of critical perspectives on how to make the changes necessary and why they were so important to make.
- The negative experience would have permeated the rest of the plant, making it difficult to recruit future team members.

With proper Notification, the Kaizen event would have felt more like a win for all of our team members.

Notification at Home

This purpose of this section is to provide examples of the application of each component (in this case, Notification) to situations other than business or manufacturing. When there are changes or expectations to reinforce, consider these strategies:

Family meetings – Meet at regular times to discuss issues and gain family alignment. Everyone has the opportunity to say what's on their mind. With love and support, everyone knows what they're expected to do and why.

Refrigerator notes – We all use the refrigerator. Critical notes can be shared there. Reduce clutter of coupons, artwork, or other things on the refrigerator, to ensure notes are easily seen.

Individual discussions with family members – Identify the key messages you want everyone to know. Sometimes a little one doesn't want the whole family there during the discussion. Communicating one-on-one reduces stress and discomfort.

Group calendars – Create a system for everyone's use. If changes are related to specific dates, put the most important information there. You know everyone will look there. If there are questions, they can be answered by the person who placed the information on the calendar.

Group texts – If you want to make sure everyone gets the same message at the same time and they're not all available, this is a viable option. In a busy world, this may be the best way to quickly deliver critical information.

One-on-one texting – Some people only respond to texts. You may not like it, but it's the world we live in. If someone needs more information, maybe they'll call or come see you, but they're just as likely to respond via text.

How to Develop Effective Notification

Four key elements create effective Notification: *what, why, how*, and *who cares*. Once you've figured those out, practice the Notification.

What – The critical information to be communicated. Lay out all of the information in a logical sequence, reduce any excess, and identify what really matters. People have short attention spans. Excess words degrade their attention. Drive out terms that don't add value until you arrive at the essence of what must be communicated.

Why – The value of the change. Why does it matter to the customer, the organization, or the people involved in the change? Does this change reduce safety risk? Does it enhance the customer experience? Will it make people's work less stressful? *Why* creates personal value and connection for those who are expected to make the change.

How – The vehicle for the communication to deliver maximum impact and alignment. Many take the easy route and gather the largest crowd possible and deliver the information. Often, this method will create more misunderstandings and errors than if you were to deliver the information personally, one-on-one. If you are willing to speak with each person individually, you must think it is critical and vital for their understanding and buy-in.

Who cares – Personalize the change in words that are meaningful from the receiver's perspective. If you do, they'll view the change as a shared responsibility. Sell yourself on the change first. Once done, you'll be able to sell it to others.

Practice – Verbalize Notification three or more times in a safe environment. The first time through identifies many improvements to make. The second time builds confidence and reveals minor improvements. The third time, you'll sound like a pro. Consider practicing with someone who will give you trusted feedback. Do they feel compelled to make the change you're describing? What other changes do they suggest?

Notification with a Language Barrier

There are times when Notification must be accomplished when there is a language barrier creating additional considerations: Who will deliver the Notification? How will it be modified to the native language of the organization? To strengthen the impact, I recommend:

- The leader most connected to the change delivers the Notification.
- Notification is communicated in the native language of the audience.
- If the leader cannot easily speak the native language, translate the Notification and/or hire a trusted interpreter.
- Encourage questions and answers to be delivered in the native language of the audience.

Mistakes to Avoid

Using email

People decide to do many things with email. They can ignore it, misinterpret it, delete it, read it, forget it, or fully understand and comply with it. Email isn't personal. It doesn't allow for strong interaction and engagement making it difficult to demonstrate your commitment to the change. Email can diminish the perception of commitment. If you're unwilling or unable to meet personally, it may appear that you don't care about the topic.

Asking someone else to notify others

If you delegate Notification to someone else, they may filter the message in a way you don't intend. If there are questions only you can answer, people will be frustrated. Your passion for the change is unlikely to be shared by the person you've delegated Notification to.

Holding large meetings

I once saw a seminar participant get up from his seat, throw down his notebook, and say, "*I can't believe I paid $4000 for this $%#!*" The reason? He was sitting in the back row of a room with many people, couldn't see the presenter, and was hard of hearing. I had paid $4000 for the same opportunity to attend. It was a positive experience for me. I was seated where I could see and hear.

When there is a large meeting, each person won't have the opportunity to ask the questions most pertinent and relevant to them. So, what do they do? They take their questions with them and attempt to answer them without any help. Human nature is to expect the worst and hope for the best. The answers they create are more likely to be negative than positive.

Video conferences

We have learned to use virtual tools as ways to improve our productivity. Video conferences have become a "*go-to*" for bringing people together from many locations. It allows people to work from home. That's the positive side of it. The negative side is that it's difficult to keep people focused, attentive, and engaged when they aren't in the same room together. There is a term called "*video conference fatigue*". If we spend too much time in video meetings, we get more tired than if we were together, in person.

We can be distracted by things going on in our lives, such as family members needing attention, the dog requiring a walk, or an interesting text coming through. When facilitating a video conference, it's challenging to manage the group. They can easily keep their distractions out of view of their webcams. It takes skill to keep everyone engaged.

Message misunderstandings

There are many stories of companies who used the wrong words for products because they didn't put the proper effort into their naming process. Some examples:

- In Ghana, there is a drink called Pee Cola. To them it means "*very good cola*". To us, not so much.
- Chevrolet made a car called Nova. It means "*doesn't go*" in Spanish. Doesn't give much confidence.
- In Poland there is a popular candy called the Fart Bar. Not sure I want a bite of that.

I'm not saying these issues are insurmountable. I am saying that you have to be thoughtful and purposeful around Notification.

How Leadership Commitment Supports Notification

Leadership Commitment is demonstrated by taking the time to share information in a meaningful way. If you believe in what you are sharing, others will too. You must know what the changes are, why they're important, and the expectations of those who will utilize them. Be unwavering in your commitment. You can't let others deviate from the new standard. The changes were developed for a purpose. They're solving a critical business problem or reducing safety risk. Leaders who participate in Notification demonstrate their commitment and the value of the changes to the organization.

Break up Notification in a way that will allow people to safely and comfortably ask questions and voice their concerns. You will create organizational alignment, understanding, and compliance.

Summary

Notification is the first spoke of the Wheel of Sustainability. It's likely the first time most of the organization will hear about the changes to be implemented. First impressions matter. How you plan and execute Notification sets the stage for the rest of the system. You are now ready to move on to the second spoke, Training and Review.

Notification Takeaways:

How strong Leadership Commitment supports Notification:

How weak Leadership Commitment damages Notification:

What I can do to improve my approach to Notification:

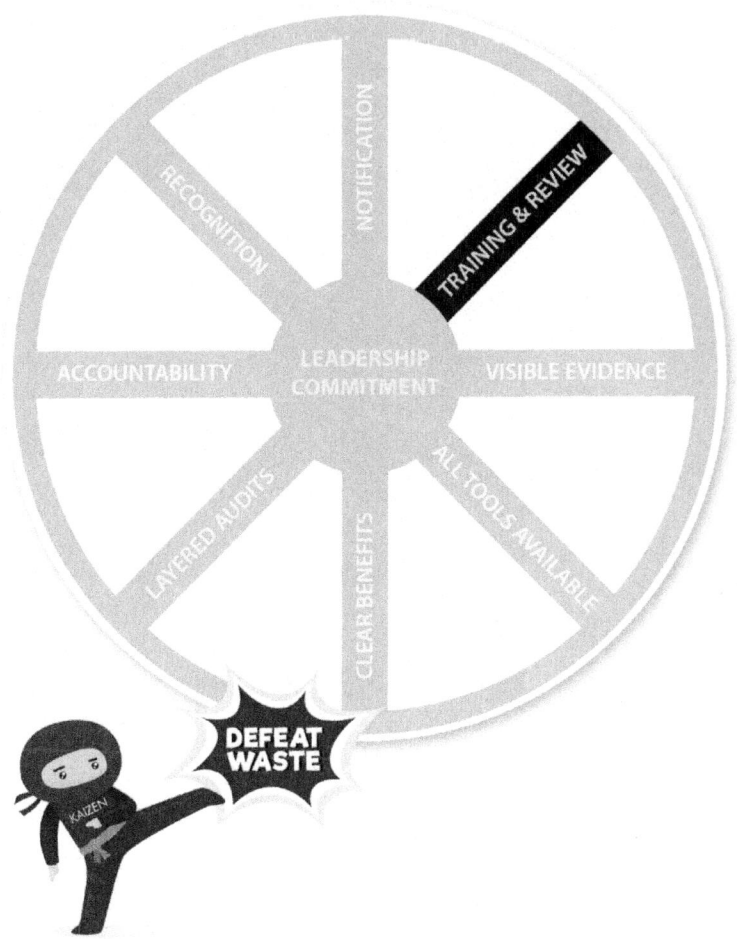

TRAINING & REVIEW

Training and Review transfers knowledge and expectations in a way that demonstrates understanding, caring, capability, and commitment to follow the changes as designed.

Introduction

Training and Review, the second spoke, provides the opportunity to deepen understanding of the changes with direct interaction between the trainer and learner. Building from the foundation of Notification, Training and Review goes deeper into the mechanics of the changes and all but guarantees functional understanding and commitment.

It helps to understand how adults retain information and learn new things, prior to getting into deeper discussion around best methods for Training and Review.

If I am standing up in front of a room explaining a change, those in the audience may retain 10 percent of the information. If some are distracted or unable to hear clearly, their specific questions may not be answered. Some may be thinking, *"all this is fine, how does it apply to me?"* Examples of other challenges when training large groups:

- Inability to address personal questions or concerns.
- Smartphones are more interesting than the topic being delivered.
- Time lag between the training and its use.

There are many other reasons to develop a more effective approach to training. Thus, this spoke of the Wheel is not called *"Training"*. There must be a way to assess understanding and compliance. Therefore, I named it Training *and* Review.

The basis for Training and Review is Training Within Industry (TWI). TWI was developed in the United States out of a critical need during World War II. Millions were drafted for the war effort, removing skilled workers from the factories. With an urgent need for production of goods, the goal was to quickly ramp up manufacturing for the United States and its allies. Less skilled workers were now in the factories. They needed to be trained quickly.

TWI was developed, increasing manufacturing capability and productivity to provide critical supplies for the fighting forces and those who remained at home. TWI used an extremely disciplined and logical methodology build standard work and to educate and train others to follow it. It's one of the reasons the United States and its allies prevailed in the war. Training and Review isn't as strict as TWI, but the general approach is the same.

I'd like to think we don't have the same sort of urgency these days. Because of global competition, disaster relief efforts, and health emergencies, organizations around the globe retool their operations with greater frequency than you might expect. Urgent or not, if you want people to truly understand and follow the changes as designed, you must have a strong approach to Training and Review.

The first step is to create as strong a connection as possible between the trainer and learner. The method to do this is Tell, Show, and Do.

Tell – The trainer tells the learner about the change and describes how it works.

Show – The trainer demonstrates the change to the learner, showing the proper way to accomplish it.

Do – The learner demonstrates their understanding by trying the change and reviewing it with the trainer.

Tell, Show, and Do is best accomplished individually or with a small group of learners in a safe environment. Questions and feedback are encouraged. Trainers demonstrate their commitment to the changes. They understand and follow them as designed. If the learner(s) deviate from standard, the trainer immediately corrects them.

It's almost impossible to ignore training if you have to demonstrate your understanding of it. During Tell, Show, and Do, the trainer provides insight and corrects the learner if there are errors or misunderstandings. The learner has the chance to ask questions and reinforce elements they aren't clear on. The bond between trainer and learner strengthens as they work together to build mutual understanding.

Training and Review is designed for changes to the job only, not the job itself. Training and Review shouldn't require hours to accomplish. If it does, it will need to be done in logical pieces. A benefit of training this way is the exposure of any weaknesses in the changes.

Principles of Training and Review

- Training and Review is delivered in a caring way.
- Training and Review is complete when understanding and commitment are demonstrated.
- The atmosphere of Training and Review must be safe and comfortable for the trainer and learner.
- Learners must demonstrate they can accomplish the changes.
- Take the time required for each individual. It's okay to have multiple attempts.
- You must be willing to expose weaknesses in the changes while delivering Training and Review. Weaknesses must be reviewed with the team that created the changes to allow them to make improvements.

Success Stories

If it Fits it Ships

I was the Quality Control Manager for a ceiling grid manufacturer. We had two plants, one in Pennsylvania and the other in Maryland, where I worked. With an eye on global expansion, plans were in place to build a new facility in France.

I was interested in the overall design and layout of the new French plant. Using my Industrial Engineering background, I felt I could help optimize the flow of materials. I was invited to participate in the development of design options prior to construction.

Working with the Maryland plant staff, we came up with what we believed was the best use of space for the six planned operating lines. We identified where raw materials would arrive and be stored. We developed finished product storage and shipping options. We minimized personnel and mobile equipment interactions. We were confident we had designed a safe and productive plant.

We were invited to the corporate headquarters to present our recommendation at an executive review of design options. During the review, it became apparent the executives favored a design that was compressed, with conflicting flows of materials and personnel.

The President proudly stated the compressed option would allow the plant to start up three months early. Only a portion of the plant would have to be built to house the operating lines. The warehouse could be built later.

I felt this design was unsafe and the plant would be hampered with poor flow for many years to come. The other executives were ready to pick the compressed design. The stress was welling up in me. My design team knew I had to voice my concerns. They looked like they thought it might be my last day with the company.

Me: "Are you willing to risk the future of the plant, just to start up three months early?"

Drew (Vice President of Engineering): "That's a pretty bold statement. Tell us what you mean about risking the future of the plant."

Me: "All six operating lines are squeezed into a space designed for three. If you look at the steel loading and finished goods packaging stations, you'll see there is no safe way for mobile equipment and personnel to service the lines when all six are running."

Drew: "Now that you mention it, something about it was bothering me too!"

Me: "Look at the end of each line. We may have to shut down when more than one needs to have materials removed. Only one forklift can fit at a time. Lines will have to sit idle, costing valuable productivity."

Drew: "I can see it now. This doesn't look like a good option to me."

The conversation in the room changed and the executive team took another look at all designs. They chose ours, with minor modifications. As we left the meeting, I felt relieved.

Months later, the plant was preparing to start production. I was asked to develop quality control drawings and provide training for the inspectors who would be checking the products being produced.

I arrived at the plant and was assigned a bi-lingual intern. My job was to teach him how ceiling grid worked, the technical details, and then design a training program for the employees. He'd translate everything into French. The first thing to do was to show him how the grid fit together.

Ceiling grid provides a structure and a framework for the ceiling tiles, lights, vents, and other accessories. The dimensions must be accurate, or the parts won't fit. The company had made some innovations to strengthen the grid, using technology called "*stitching*."

Stitching joins the metal together in such a way that it stays straight and doesn't flex when it's installed. The *stitching* also makes the metal act as if it's thicker. Holes in the grid allow other grid components to be inserted and connected at ninety-degree angles.

I started at the beginning with the intern. Placing a twelve-foot bar of grid on the floor of the plant, I told him to imagine it was up in the ceiling. Then I showed him how the first four-foot bar of grid was designed to go through the hole in the twelve-foot bar. Next, I told him, "Now, we put the connecting four-foot bar of grid through the hole to meet up with the other four-foot bar like this …. like this …" They were both supposed to fit through the same hole and connect to each other. They didn't. What was wrong?

We turned one of the four-foot bars around and were able to connect both bars through the hole. We tested more grid and determined one out of every three connections didn't work, an unacceptable scrap rate. We had to figure out what was happening. If the *stitching* was on the ends of both pieces of grid, it made the connection thicker than the width of the hole and the grid couldn't fit. We had to figure out how to remove the *stitching* from the ends of the grid. Otherwise, we were out of business.

How did the *stitching* get on the ends of the grid, I wondered? It wasn't on any of the quality control drawings. Or was it? I hadn't identified this critical issue when I was developing the drawings. To make matters worse, no one had tried to put any of the grid together prior to my arrival. If any of the grid had been shipped, it would be a customer relations disaster. My heart sank to my stomach.

It turns out this was the day the first shipment of grid was being shipped to a customer. There was a celebration in the plant with speeches, cheering, and champagne. At a break in the festivities, I took the Plant Manager aside and told him what we found. We had to bring the shipment back to the plant in order to assess the situation, protect the customer, the reputation of the company, and the new plant. He looked unhappy, but understood and supported the plan. Luckily, the truck was still on the road and hadn't reached the customer.

The following day, we determined how to remove the *stitching* from the ends of the grid and the problem was solved. All production was stopped until the issue was resolved. We used that time to train the staff and production workers on grid quality control and mechanics.

Using Tell, Show, and Do, everyone was given a chance to become a grid installer. We showed them how things were supposed to work and then what happens when things don't work. All quality control drawings were modified to show where the *stitching* was supposed to be. The areas it wasn't supposed to be were highlighted.

After a two-day production delay, new grid was produced to take the place of the defective product. The plant was successful for many years following this initial issue. Rushing into production would have had devastating effects for the company. Taking the time to analyze the process and try things out spared the company significant losses and damage to its reputation and credibility.

One-on-one Training and Review sessions are the most effective way to share information and engage learners. In large organizations, this can feel unwieldy and feels like a huge amount of effort. The issue is resolved when the organization identifies multiple trainers. In this next story, a Kaizen team found a way to leverage training across its team members.

Training in the Moment

I was hired to help a gummy vitamin manufacturer in Washington State reduce their changeover time. Walking through the process with my Sponsor, I was confident we could achieve a sustainable 50 percent reduction in time, improve the safety of the process, and give the team a winning experience.

Changeover

Switching from one product to another. For example, a production line is building a blue car. The next product is a red pickup truck. Many processes and materials will have to be changed to build the next product, including paint and body style.

Changeover time

The time it takes from the last good product of the previous run (car) to the first good product of the following run (truck).

After the problem statement and objectives for the Kaizen event were developed, we identified the team. We included people who work in the process, those who manage the process, and others who were interested in helping the team win. Two team members from an East Coast location joined us as well.

On the first day of the Kaizen, the team was joined by a group of observers from management and other staff. They were interested in what was about to happen. After introductions, an engineer, who was not on the team, voiced his concerns about reducing changeover time by half without substantial capital investment or weeks of training.

Having facilitated dozens of changeover reduction Kaizen events with consistent success, I stated we wouldn't have to spend much money and everyone would be properly trained by the end of the week. I told them every team before them was able to achieve their time reduction goal and I was confident they would too. Team members looked skeptical, but were willing to give it a try. Management voiced support for the team.

The average changeover took four hours and thirty minutes. Our goal was to safely complete a changeover in less than two hours and fifteen minutes by the end of the week. After an initial review of changeover reduction techniques and Lean principles, we walked out to the factory floor and observed the crew on shift conducting a changeover. It took them five hours and thirty-two minutes. After the changeover was complete, we returned to the meeting room to share observations and ideas for improvement. At the end of a long first day, we had prioritized three improvement projects:

1.   Modify equipment to simplify the changeover and reduce safety risk.
2.   Create visuals to error-proof and coordinate procedures.
3.   Optimize tool placement.

We went to dinner to unwind and continue the discussion. Even though it was a long day, team members were excited about what might be possible.

On the morning of the second day, we started to make the prioritized changes. The plan was to implement as many improvements as possible in the morning, with team members conducting the modified changeover in the afternoon.

This time, the crew on shift would observe the team, rather than the other way around. Some basic organization, visualization, and minor equipment improvements were made before lunchtime. We were now ready to test our changes.

We planned to review our results and ideas immediately following the changeover. It was critical for team learning and new improvement ideas. Team members agreed to stay late.

The team completed the changeover in five hours and three minutes. They looked tired and uninterested in staying any longer. Undeterred, I brought them back to the meeting room and reviewed their feedback.

Doug, a supervisor on the team, pointed out while individuals had simpler and safer methods to do their work, there was no coordination of effort between the six team members. This was a revelation. Doug was enthusiastic to build something we could try the next day. The team was spent and went home.

Day three started with a flurry of activity. Doug and a few others came together to develop ways to coordinate efforts during the changeover. A four-foot by eight-foot white board was repurposed to track the activities of team members and display status before and during the changeover. It wasn't completed before our next test. We decided to start using it anyway to see what we'd learn.

Using the new board and other improvements from the morning, the team completed the changeover in three hours and seventeen minutes. Team members were excited about their results and what might be possible. No one remembered completing a changeover in less than three and a half hours. Their goal was in sight.

Before the team left for the day, I told them we would be asking the crew to try the new changeover procedure on the fourth day. This meant we had to complete all improvements and train the crew. Now the team was nervous. How would they train people who had never seen our new procedure in such a short amount of time? I assured them we would be just fine. They weren't as confident.

The team arrived on day four, wondering how to transfer all changes to the crew to use after lunch. I explained Tell, Show, and Do. Each team member would pair up with a crew member one hour before starting our next changeover preparation and test.

They would first Tell their partner about the new procedure. Next, they would Show how to do it. Finally, they would have their partner Do the procedure to demonstrate their understanding. This technique would bring out questions and create rapid understanding. Team members were encouraged to consider this new training approach as they were working on their improvement projects.

By lunchtime, all improvement work was complete. The white board was upgraded to show status of each task for each of the six crew members in "*swim lanes*". The Shift Coordinator managed the white board. There was a timeline from two hours before the changeover was to start (preparation steps) to three hours from the changeover start, in thirty-minute segments. The idea was to complete every preparation step before shutting the line down. Then, every changeover step was to be completed in less than three hours across all six *swim lanes*.

Every step had a red magnet on it. When the step was completed, the Shift Coordinator was to remove the red magnet and replace it with a green one. If one of the crew members was green in their *swim lane* while another crew member was red, the Shift Coordinator could ask them to help whoever was behind.

We assembled the crew and team before the training was about to begin. We thanked the crew for participating and told them the team was doing their best to make this the safest, easiest changeover possible. Team members would pair up with them to show all of the changes.

We asked the crew members to try everything in the new way, as safely as possible. We'd get their feedback following the changeover. If they thought anything was unsafe, they should determine a safe way to complete the step and we'd make the appropriate changes afterwards. Crew members asked questions and then indicated they were ready to try the new changeover procedure.

Training started and everyone paired up and walked around the area, discussing and trying the changes. The white board was placed prominently in front of the supervisor's office. Everyone could see the board from where they were working.

After the training was complete, changeover preparation began. The line was still running. Crew members had to watch the line as well as complete their preparation steps. Team members shadowed the crew members and coached them in the new procedure. They were not allowed to assist or do the work for them.

Back at the white board, Vince, the Line Leader, and Julio, the Shift Coordinator, were turning some of the red magnets green, as preparation steps were completed. One of the crew members was getting far ahead of the others.

Me: "Hey guys, the white board seems to be helping you coordinate the changeover."

Julio: "We've never been able to see it this way. I think it's going to be useful."

Me: "Based on what I am seeing, it looks like there are some opportunities to help the crew. What is the white board telling you?"

Julio: "I'm not sure what you mean."

Me: "Swim Lane Three has many green magnets in it."

Vince: "Yeah, that's Donna. She's a good worker and knows what she's doing. She's way ahead."

Me: "Now, look at Swim Lane Five."

Julio: "Oh, that's Alex. He's pretty new. With all of those red magnets, he's getting behind."

Me: "Is there something we can do about that?"

Julio: "I definitely think we could. Let us discuss it a bit."

Julio and Vince clearly had no idea how to use this new tool. Even though we had reviewed the white board prior to starting the changeover, there hadn't been a complete Tell, Show, and Do.

I assumed the use of the board was self-explanatory. It wasn't, at least not yet. Julio and Vince were back in their original mindset to let people do their work and finish when they finish, without getting help. I couldn't leave it at that. This was too big of an opportunity.

Me: "What do you think you could do to help Alex?"

Julio: "I'm not sure. What do you think Vince?"

Vince: "I'm not sure either."

Me: "This is our chance to see if the board improves our changeovers. We could let Donna help Alex until he gets back on track."

Vince: "That makes sense to me."

I left them, hoping they would take the initiative to get help for Alex. Three minutes later, they hadn't left the board. Donna was getting further ahead.

Me: "Are you going to get help for Alex?"

Julio: "Definitely. We will in a minute."

I left, but didn't go far. Julio and Vince were still talking at the board. I went back to the board and said, "Let's go see Donna and ask her to help Alex."

They grudgingly walked with me up to the mezzanine, where Donna was working. I introduced myself to her and explained my role as facilitator.

Me: "You're doing such a great job with this new changeover procedure that you're way ahead of schedule."

Donna: "Thanks. I didn't realize I was."

Me: "Since you're so far ahead, would you mind helping Alex? He's getting pretty far behind and could use some help."

Donna: "I'd be happy to. Alex is a good guy and we work well together."

Me: "Thanks Donna. Let's go see Alex."

Donna: "Hey Alex, do you want some help? I'm ahead and it looks like I could get you back on track."

Alex: "You mean it? Wow, I could really use some help. Thanks Donna."

Vince and Julio experienced a light bulb moment. They made more moves to drive Red tasks to Green. Once they understood Tell and Show, they were able to Do.

Another team member found a large computer monitor and placed it in the window of the supervisor's office, with the screen facing out towards the crew and team members. He set it up to be a large timer for everyone to see.

The timer was started the moment the line was shut down for changeover. Everyone could see how long it was taking. Back at the white board, every time a red magnet was switched to green, Vince and Julio high-fived. There was no way the team would fail now.

As we approached the two-hour mark, it looked like we might meet our goal. People started to get excited. Julio was making all of the moves he could to ensure a win for the team. At two hours and five minutes there was cheering and clapping. Everyone thought they were done. It was a false alarm. The Quality Department had not yet signed off on the new product being produced and wasn't in the area.

Vince walked rapidly to the Quality Office to get a representative to look at the product and do the required quality checks. At two hours and ten minutes, all approvals were received. There was a roar of applause and a bunch of hugging that I doubt ever happened before in the plant.

The crew and team returned to the meeting room to provide feedback. No one thought what we had accomplished would be possible. They now realized it was. They understood the importance of coordination, help, and coaching. The team agreed to train all of the other crew members using Tell, Show, and Do. In this way, they could ensure full understanding and buy-in for the new changeover procedure.

On the day of the report-out, each team member admitted they didn't think we'd be able to reach our goal. It was hard not to say, "*I told you so!*" If I were to pick the most important changes they made, it would be the coordination, visualization, and Tell, Show, and Do. Everyone knew what they had to do to win.

Lean in action

I was responsible for the Lean transformation for the Global Technology group at a ceiling tile manufacturer for six years. I delivered Lean training to all employees when they joined our group. The goal was to help them understand how Lean applied to our work. My aim was to generate interest and engagement. In the early years, things didn't always go as expected.

When I first started training new employees, I created eighty PowerPoint slides that described as many Lean concepts as I could squeeze into the two hours allotted for the training. I reviewed the slides, gave participants a chance to ask questions, and then declared them "*trained*". There weren't many questions. New employee participation in Lean efforts was hit or miss once the training was completed.

I knew I had to do better to realize some challenging engagement and participation goals. The first thing I did was develop activities to demonstrate various Lean concepts. From an interactive 5S number search to a triangle peg jumping game, new employees started to draw value from their training time. Engagement and participation slightly increased. What else could be done, I wondered?

The breakthrough came one day when a new employee asked, "This is all well and good, but how does it apply to what we do in Global Technology?" I now knew what I had to do: make the training specific to our work and demonstrate *Lean in action.*

The first thing I did was test the training against our department Vision and Mission. If the training didn't support it directly, it was modified. The theoretical became practical. PowerPoint slides were reduced and made more relevant.

Focusing on the suggestion of *Lean in action*, a Gemba walk was added. After an hour of classroom review (Tell), we toured areas that had applied Lean thinking to their processes. From the Pilot Plant to the Capital Engineering Records Room to the New Product Development Project Board, new employees could observe (Show) and interact (Do) with people using Lean. They had a clearer image of how it worked in practical settings.

Training still took two hours. It was more interactive, engaging, and received positive reviews from the participants. I enjoyed it more too. Most importantly, Lean participation and engagement of new employees rose to record levels.

Less than Success Story

We Won the Battle but Lost the War

During my corporate career, we identified a critical gap in our safety training system. There wasn't a good way to ensure traveling engineers, scientists, and technicians were compliant for annual safety training requirements. We had to get everyone immediately compliant and then develop a system for annual recertification.

Working with a small team and under the direction of the Global Technical Services Vice President, we established "*Technical Services Safety Days*". No one was allowed to travel during the week of training.

We developed interactive safety training activities that included everyone in the group. This would allow us to achieve compliance and provide useful skills for work and at home. We added some fun activities and games to encourage team building and networking. When training wasn't occurring, employees were encouraged to catch up on paperwork and reconnect with others at the corporate center.

Technical Services Safety Days was a success. One hundred and fifty employees learned and practiced firefighting, equipment lock-out, chemical hazard identification, and many other critical safety topics. Tell, Show, and Do was used extensively. People appreciated the personal touches throughout the experience. My team won an award for putting together this meaningful activity and restoring safety compliance in short order.

For the next three years, *Technical Services Safety Days* was an annual event. People looked forward to it. Everyone blocked out their calendars for the week. For some, it was their only time in the office and they took advantage of the opportunity to network with their co-workers. They honed their skills through the creative training of best safety practices.

Then, everything changed. The company purchased a computer-based system to deliver required safety training. Employees could review the training on their own time and at their own pace during the year.

Except, it really didn't work that way. Most waited until the end of the year and then crammed the training in to get it done. There was little engagement or knowledge retention. It seemed like a good idea and a better use of resources, but in the end, we lost the immeasurable value of having interactive *Technical Services Safety Days*.

Training and Review at Home

I am very fortunate to have a wife who enjoys cooking. Peggy has a broad repertoire. I look forward to every meal. She didn't learn to be a great cook overnight. She had a lot of help and strong Training and Review.

Growing up with three brothers and one sister, Peggy wanted to contribute to the family. She helped out on the farm and in the kitchen. Her grandmother, father, and mother alternated cooking duties. Her earliest memories of learning to cook were with her grandmother, who taught her how to make biscuits. She was six at the time.

Her grandmother first told her about the art of making biscuits (Tell). Next, she was shown how to make the biscuits, which were a daily staple (Show). Now, it was time for her to demonstrate she could make biscuits (Do). With her grandmother beside her, Peggy carefully added ingredients. She was told to "put in a little more" of this or that. She then mixed the ingredients.

With help, she put the biscuits in the oven. Initial feedback was favorable, but the biscuits were a little "*tough*". Her grandmother showed her how to handle the biscuits less before putting them in the oven. From then on, she was the official biscuit maker.

Peggy's cooking skills grew through the years. By the time she was thirteen, she was the official family cook on weeknights. I don't think that was her original intent, but I'm definitely reaping the rewards for all of her efforts and skills.

How to Develop Effective Training and Review

Training and Review must be aligned and reinforce the message shared during Notification, the first spoke of the Wheel of Sustainability. Don't send mixed messages or create confusion about what is right. Follow these steps to achieve the best results while conducting Training and Review for key changes.

Before Conducting Training and Review

Set aside time to Train and Review without distractions. Plan more time than you think you'll need. Nobody ever complained when a meeting ended early.

Decide whether you will train one person at a time or a small group of learners. If more learners are to be included, consider engaging another trainer to help.

Describe what you're about to do. Most people aren't familiar with Tell, Show, and Do. You don't want to surprise anyone with expectations of their involvement. The following is an example of how I introduce Tell, Show, and Do:

"I'm about to review changes with you using a technique called 'Tell, Show, and Do.' I'll tell you about the changes, show you how they impact you, and then ask you to demonstrate your understanding of them. I do this to get your input and ensure you have the best opportunity to understand and follow the changes created for our benefit. Feel free to stop me at any time and ask questions. Hold me accountable to train you to the point where you're confident and can easily follow the new procedure."

Determine how you will review the changes in a way that is non-destructive to the process. Do you have to stop a production line, meeting, computer system, or other activity to accomplish Training and Review? Can you demonstrate changes without directly impacting the process in question?

If you choose to use Training Within Industry as your model for Training and Review, I recommend you do further research. I don't presume to be an expert and can't do it justice in this small space. I am including a reference below[2]. If you want to know more about my approach, read on.

Tell

What to do – During Notification, the organization learned about the changes to be implemented. Now, you will describe what they are in context with the work to be accomplished. *You aren't teaching people all aspects of their jobs.* Identify the changes affecting their normal job and highlight only those. What are the interactions, differences, enhancements and safety risks mitigated by the changes?

---

[2] Misiurek, Bartosz. *Standardized Work with TWI: Eliminating Human Errors in Production and Service Processes.* Productivity Press, 2016.

How to do it – What are the steps required? What is the best order of the steps? What tools, techniques, visuals, documentation, jigs, fixtures, computer programs, or other devices are to be used in following the steps? Are there ergonomic or other safety best practices to be followed during the tasks?

Why do it – What are the benefits of the changes as they relate to the normal tasks? Why did the team come to the conclusion the changes are beneficial? Why does the team believe the changes make the task(s) safer, simpler, less stressful, and/or more productive?

Seek questions – Did the learner grasp all that you've covered? Ask open-ended questions to verify they were paying attention and understand the basics of what you've reviewed thus far. If they don't understand, take the time to repeat key points.

Show

Demonstrate steps in the *exact sequence* and approach as designed. Practice, practice, practice until you are comfortable. If you do it wrong, admit the mistake and start over again. The key here is the learner must be able to visualize performing the change and you need to show the way. Follow this sequence for Show:

Slow speed demonstration – Speak the changes as you are following the procedure. Stop for questions, especially at critical points. Make sure the learner understands the differences in procedure and the reasons before moving on. Help the learner visualize the benefits through your demonstration. Point out the safety, productivity, and other improvements as you arrive at them. Ask for questions at the end of the demonstration. If there's more than one learner, make sure you give everyone the opportunity to ask questions. If someone is not asking questions, ask questions of them.

Comfortable (normal) speed demonstration – You must be able to show changes are possible at a comfortable and safe speed. During this part of the demonstration, only the most critical elements should be verbalized. At the end of the demonstration, ask for questions.

Repeat, as necessary – Does one normal speed demonstration do the trick, or are there elements to be shown again? Allow extra time, don't rush, and make the learner comfortable to ask for another review if needed. Watch body language. Is the learner engaged? Are they just trying to get through this and move on to their normal job? You are accountable for their understanding as much as they are. Make the effort to reach them. If you are unable to achieve engagement, don't be afraid to ask what you can do to help. If you're stuck, ask someone to help you with the review.

Ask for questions – What was learned through the demonstration? What was confusing? Do they see the changes as beneficial? If so, how? If not, why not? Ask open-ended questions to confirm understanding.

Do

It's time for the learner(s) to demonstrate their understanding. Before they try the changes, give them another chance to ask questions. Next, ask them to describe what they are about to do. If they are confused or unclear, it's time to go back to Tell and Show, or at least clarify the changes once again. If there is more than one learner, focus on one at a time. Do not move on to the next learner until the first one is fully competent and comfortable.

Learner describes what they're going to do – Before demonstrating their understanding, this is an opportunity to ascertain comfort with the changes. You can quickly identify any gaps, before a full demonstration.

Slow speed demonstration - Ask the learner to follow the change sequence at a slow speed, and with no discussion of what's being done, unless you need to clarify details. Remind them it's the first time through and mistakes are expected and encouraged; it's how people learn. Take note of the mistakes or issues with sequence or technique. Do not interrupt, unless the learner is putting themself or someone else at risk. After this first attempt, allow time for input, questions, concerns, or anything else to be resolved prior to the next attempt.

Comfortable (normal) speed demonstration - Once the learner has shown competence at slow speed, ask them to try it again at normal speed. This is the opportunity to get comfortable with the changes at their pace. Watch for any issues during this demonstration, especially steps out of sequence or not using the tools, visuals, documents, or other components of the change developed to ensure the best possible experience. Review issues immediately.

If you're not comfortable with this demonstration, ask the learner to do it again, with identified corrections. You may need to demonstrate a critical element again. Regardless, don't end this effort until you both are comfortable with the understanding and commitment to the changes.

Ask for questions – Now that the learner has demonstrated competence, it should be easy to address concerns, issues, or gather input on improvements.

After

Follow up with your learners to reinforce understanding and commitment to the changes. Showing your commitment to the changes goes a long way in successful implementation (Leadership Commitment). Set a time to check in and verify things are going as they should. As time goes by, you can reduce frequency of check-ins. These changes are critical. They must be followed. Frequent and strong follow-up strengthens overall commitment.

Mistakes to Avoid

Training a large group all at once

As with Notification, the less engaging the Training and Review, the less likely the learners will retain and follow the new process or procedure. There is no opportunity to confirm understanding or engage in deep question and answer sessions. Unfortunately, most training happens this way. Put many people in a room, present a bunch of PowerPoint slides and declare they're "*trained*". It's happened to me as a learner and I've done it as a trainer. You've probably done it too.

Training on a computer

This method saves money, allows people to get the training when they have time for it, and take the time they need to understand what they're learning. In many cases, this isn't what actually happens. People go through the information as a fill-in to other work. They don't have an opportunity to review what they're learning with others. They can be easily distracted. Some software platforms are sophisticated enough to verify understanding, but people can "*game the system*." How will they demonstrate their understanding if no one is there to coach and guide them?

Rushing Training and Review

Each person learns at their own pace. They must feel safe and comfortable. If you don't set aside enough time, they won't have the opportunity to address their issues and you won't have enough time to coach and correct them.

Using virtual training

Learners can attend training from any location around the world. The trainer can engage with them. The disadvantage is that it will be challenging to watch them demonstrate their understanding. While individual questions or issues are being raised, others wait for their questions to be answered. They may tune out or disengage.

How Leadership Commitment Supports Training and Review

Training and Review takes time. There will be much one-on-one training to ensure everyone has the opportunity to ask questions and understand the changes. Leadership must provide the time and resources to allow for a deep and thorough Training and Review. It must support and be aligned with Notification. Leaders hold the team accountable to implement the two spokes in a way that will enhance organizational understanding and commitment.

There will be times when members of the leadership team will be asked questions about the changes. Leadership Commitment is demonstrated by applying Tell, Show, and Do. If you know and review the *how* and the *why*, and then require others to demonstrate their understanding, they will value the importance of the changes.

Summary

Training and Review shows people how much you care about them. You take time out of your day to ensure they do the right thing in the safest and most productive way. You demonstrate your commitment to the changes by showing you are willing and able to follow the new process or procedure. You show your vulnerability as you follow the new steps and utilize the new methods. You are open to the direct questions and feedback from those you train. You are taking whatever time it takes for each individual you interact with. You are giving a gift to your co-worker(s) by keeping them safe and productive.

The first two spokes of the Wheel of Sustainability focus on how changes are communicated and reinforced with those who will be directly affected by them. The next two spokes focus on the tools and systems developed to ensure people will have everything they need to carry out the changes in the safest and most productive way.

Training and Review Takeaways:

How strong Leadership Commitment supports Training and Review:

How weak Leadership Commitment damages Training and Review:

What I can do to improve my approach to Training and Review:

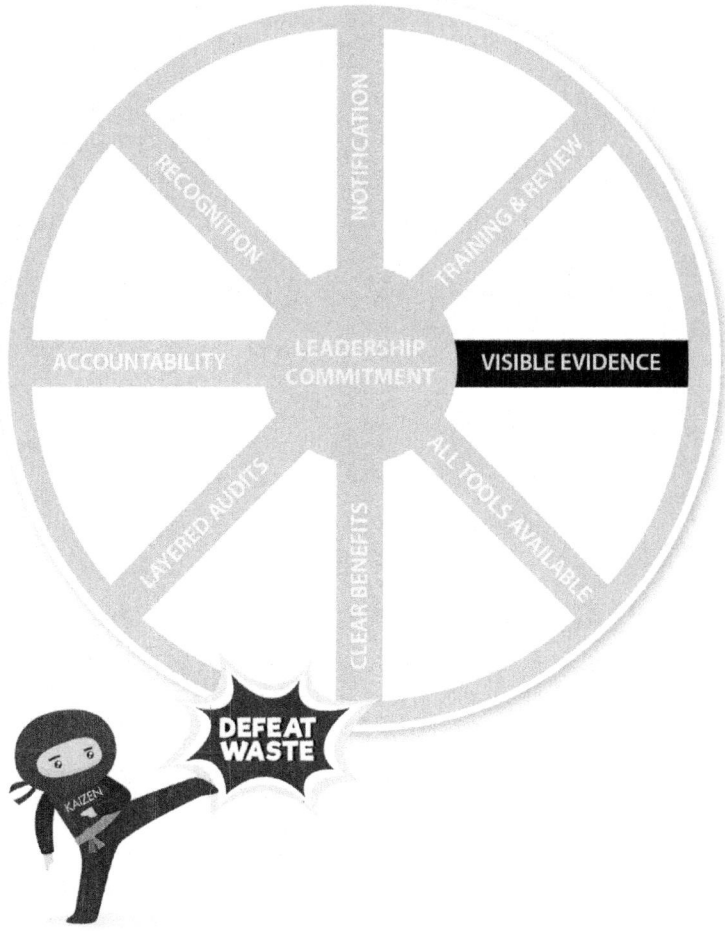

VISIBLE EVIDENCE

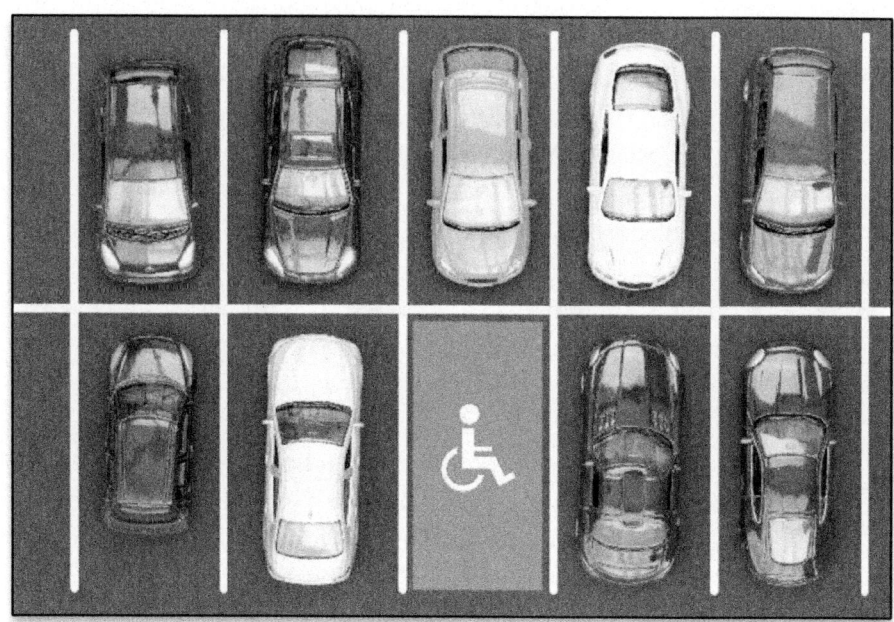

Visible Evidence allows anyone to assess the health of a system and makes it almost impossible to do the wrong thing.

Introduction

Visible Evidence is the third spoke of the Wheel of Sustainability. Its aim is to create visuals reinforcing the changes that are well thought out and logically placed. The result is people will be helped to do the right thing without expending extra effort.

We often assume others understand our intent, meaning, or the details we're reviewing. It's not always a valid assumption. People are busy, easily distracted, forgetful, or not as excited about the topic as we may be. Systems must be developed to make it almost *impossible to do the wrong thing* when implementing a change. Visible Evidence supports the development of those systems.

I used to have challenging conversations with a co-worker about putting up signs in a testing facility. He believed there were too many signs there already. Every time I wanted to improve signage, he was concerned I was just adding more visual clutter and people wouldn't pay attention. He was right to a point. His concern was that putting up signs for the sake of signs wouldn't be effective. Eventually, they'd be ignored and lose their meaning.

I felt I was displaying helpful information, not just more signs. He wasn't convinced. His frame of reference came from prior experience with visuals placed indiscriminately in other areas. Eventually, we came to the understanding that signs created with a purpose were beneficial.

Examples of visuals that don't help people do the right thing:

- A banner hanging over a product inspection station in Georgia – "Employees will not sleep. Employees will not pass defective products to the customer. Employees will not violate safety rules." Seems a bit insulting to me. No, *really,* I want to sleep at the inspection station.
- A sign posted at the time clock and seen by all employees in a factory in Kentucky – "Drug sales or use on premises will lead to arrest and prosecution" Not a great morale booster. Is there *somewhere else* I can sell or use drugs that won't lead to my arrest?

Visible Evidence directs us to create purposeful and useful visuals. In this way, there can't be too many. The rest of the chapter is intended to help you design and implement the proper Visible Evidence to help people *do the right thing at all times.*

The Twenty-Foot Rule

Have you ever driven to the mall and wondered why some people are parked improperly? How were you able to tell? Parking lots are designed so that people can assess the situation from far away. Drivers make decisions before arriving at their parking spots. They may ask:

- Is there a parking place near the entrance of the store?
- Do I want to park near someone who isn't between the lines?
- What's my best chance of avoiding damage to my car when I park?

I named the principle used to design parking lots the Twenty-foot Rule. Status of an area must be easily determined from twenty feet away or more.

I challenge teams I work with to use the Twenty-foot Rule and create Visible Evidence to support and sustain the changes they are implementing. Visuals must be simple, easy to interpret, and observable from a distance. The team should agree on the meanings of the visuals and design them in a way to help people do the right thing at all times. Deviations must be obvious. Leaders must then commit to helping correct deviations from the standard.

The effectiveness of the Visible Evidence is tested by asking: *How do I know?* Assess an area, process, or procedure and ask:

- How do I know everything is as it should be?
- How do I know if there is something going wrong?
- How do I know people know what to do?
- How do I know people have everything they need to do their job safely, productively, and in the best possible manner?

Teams are challenged to develop visuals to answer *How do I know?* questions from twenty feet away. Visuals must be simple, easy to see from any location, require little or no explanation (i.e., a young child would understand what's going on), and identify status quickly. As an example, the colors red and green indicate status. Green means everything is fine. Red means help is needed.

Visible Evidence supports the critical changes to be implemented. The changes have already been defined. The visuals should be placed in the locations where they will create a connection between the change required, the proper way it is to be done, and the result to be achieved. It's not unusual to place the same visuals in multiple locations, within easy sight of the person doing the work or the person responsible for it. Examples are:

- Settings on a dial that are divided into red, yellow, and green sections.

- Performance parameters displayed on a large monitor.
- The scoreboard at a baseball game.
- The position of a handle that indicates a valve is open or closed.
- The location of a tool or other piece of equipment.
- The proper setup of a workstation.
- The layout of a computer program.

Once the visuals have been defined, use 5S thinking to optimize their organization and placement.

5S Thinking

Lean practitioners use 5S to organize spaces and make them safer and more productive. Although many great manufacturing organizations have been credited with inventing or popularizing 5S, I'm pretty sure my mother invented it!

When I was young, I wasn't very organized. My mother told me, "pick up your clothes," "put your toys away," "make your bed," and most importantly, *"there's a place for everything and everything in its place."* Not only did she tell me to do these things, she showed me how to do them, nagged me about them, and frequently checked my work. I couldn't get away with anything.

I didn't always follow my mother's advice as a child. As I grew older, I came to realize how powerful her statements were. When I started my career, I applied 5S thinking to my work and was amazed at the immediate positive impact I was able to make. I also saw how deeply it moved those who participated in 5S efforts. They became disciples of the approach, and wouldn't allow others to erode any of its benefits.

As simple and powerful as 5S is, there are many who don't understand what it is and how it should be used. To them, it's an excuse to clean things up. It's so much more than that.

The purpose of 5S is to improve the safety and productivity of an area or work space. Once agreement and alignment around this purpose is established, the team uses 5S to provide this benefit to users of the area.

The 5S's are:

1. Sort
2. Set in Order
3. Shine
4. Standardize
5. Sustain

Implement 5S in order. Highest value is attained when all are implemented as a system.

Sort

Remove anything not immediately needed or useful in the area. Duplication, clutter, and non-working items are removed, discarded, donated, or sold. Three hammers become one, broken things are disposed of or repaired. Things saved *"just in case,"* are no longer allowed in the area. It's not unusual to remove more than 80 percent of the tools, materials, documents, and other things. Productivity is improved by reducing the time and effort required to find and use what's needed. Safety is improved, as there is no need to move clutter out of the way to accomplish work. Once Sort is complete, move on to Set in Order.

Set in Order

Create visible, easy to find locations for all remaining materials, tools, and equipment. Define proper inventory levels, and place everything within reach. Make it impossible to lose anything. Take as much off of the floor as possible. Follow Mom's advice: *A place for everything and everything in its place.* Safety is improved through the elimination of trip and bump hazards. Productivity continues to improve as it becomes easier to be compliant to system requirements. Shine is next.

Shine

Clean and inspect remaining items to ensure they're in optimal condition. Problems are prevented by identification and resolution of issues, cracks, leaks, or poor performance. Do this *before* there is a need for tools, equipment, documents or other things to accomplish work. Some people think Shine means to *"clean things up."* It's much more than that. Shine reduces the risk of failure, greatly improving productivity. Safety is enhanced because things work properly when called upon. There are no surprises. All physical changes have been made, now it's time to build a system to keep everything in top shape. Continue to Standardize.

Standardize

Set expectations and create audits to keep things as they should be. It's no longer the responsibility of only one person. The greater organization provides support. Someone working in the area may not realize things are shifting to their prior condition, removed items are starting to return, or people aren't following the rules. An auditor will. Create Visible Evidence of *what good looks like* so the system can be quickly and easily assessed.

Now, there's a better chance to catch issues quickly and create accountability to follow the rules of the area. In the context of my childhood, I thought my room was okay every day. My mother didn't see it that way. She frequently pointed out the error of my thinking.

Safety and productivity gains are maintained through Leadership Commitment to the organization and its auditors. Are we done at the fourth S? You would think so. But wait, there's one more S: Sustain.

Sustain

The organization is challenged to continually improve the performance of the area. By keeping score and tracking it for everyone to see, further improvements are identified. Once an area has seen the benefit of implementing 5S, it's not unusual for people to identify other areas that could use it (Recognition).

I think we can all agree being organized is beneficial. I think we also can agree we should listen to our mothers more often. They are very wise, indeed.

Make it almost impossible to do the wrong thing

5S sets the stage for creating Visible Evidence that makes it *almost impossible to do the wrong thing*. After clutter is removed from the area during Sort, the team identifies the best way to arrange the remaining materials using Set in Order. Once the arrangement is agreed to, the Visible Evidence of the status of the process may be optimized. Here's an example:

A critical wrench is used to safely maintain equipment in the area. The wrench must be easy to find, safe to use, obvious in its use and condition, and simple to return to its home location. The first step is to pick the proper wrench:

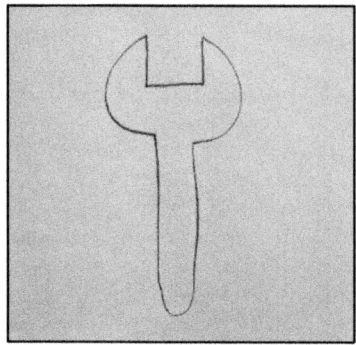

Ask the question: How Do I Know it's the correct wrench? The answer is: we don't know, until it's identified:

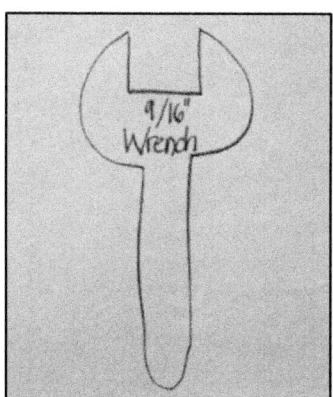

The next question is: How Do I Know where the wrench came from? If the wrench is taken out of the area and misplaced, there's no way to know where it came from. Label its home location:

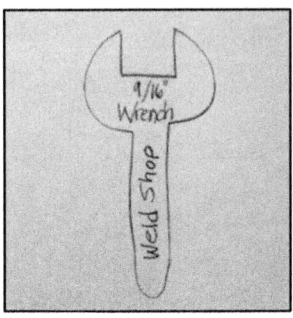

Now we know it came from the Weld shop. Question three is: How Do I Know where to return the wrench in the Weld shop? Once the optimal location is identified, draw an outline for the wrench:

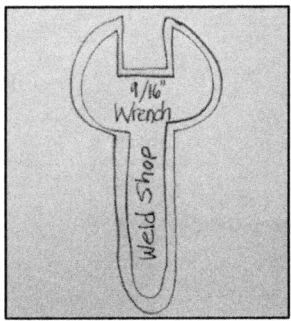

The final question is: How Do I Know this is the proper location for the $\frac{9}{16}$" wrench? Add the required information to the outline and the process is complete:

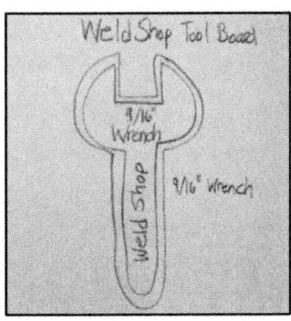

It's *almost impossible* to lose the wrench. If it's found in another area, the label will indicate it belongs in the Weld shop. Once returned to the Weld shop, its final location is obvious. If you're concerned tools will go missing, consider using this approach.

There are many other ways to achieve similar results. Color coding, striping, naming, and other creative techniques help people do the right thing. It's best to let the team or the Area Owner define the method to ensure tools never go missing. Use *How Do I Know?* questions to verify the visuals create the desired result and help people do the right thing every time.

Principles of Visible Evidence

- Anyone can assess the health of the operating system. They know when they need to provide help.
- Status can easily be determined from twenty feet away.
- Visuals are designed in a way that it's almost impossible to do the wrong thing.
- Information is convenient to those doing the work.
- Leaders go to the information. They don't make it come to them.

Success Stories

Lead from the Front – The Story of the Pink Tools

The global ceiling tile manufacturer I worked for started their Lean journey many years ago. At the onset, they brought in consultants, who facilitated and guided Kaizen events and coached leaders at every manufacturing site around the world. Our fiberglass ceiling tile plant in Ohio had a strong culture of teamwork and employee engagement.

Early on, the plant didn't have an internal leader for their Lean journey. Having just completed an assignment as Production Manager in Oregon, I was asked to act as the interim Lean Leader for the plant.

I had worked with Steve, the Plant Manager, years before at the corporate office. At that time, he was the Manager of Technology Resourcing. I reported to him for two years and we got along well. Soft spoken and strongly principled, Steve had the proper mindset to sponsor the plant Lean transformation.

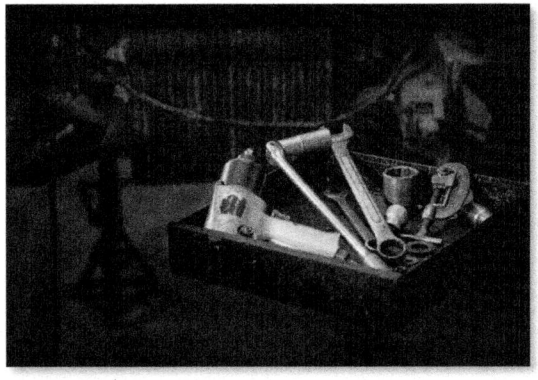

The plant conducted a Value Stream Mapping (VSM) event and set their overall Lean strategy. They identified and scheduled many Kaizen events in the months following the VSM. The first one was a 5S event on a critical production line. I was asked to facilitate.

Steve and I chartered the event and chose the strongest, most engaged team we could to ensure our first Kaizen would be a win. Top line operators, mechanics, and support staff dedicated five days to drive breakthrough safety and productivity improvements for the line.

In the early days of our Lean journey, facilitators were required to use the entire first day of the Kaizen to train the team. The idea was to make team members comfortable by spending extra time teaching Lean principles and tools.

Line operators and mechanics don't have much tolerance for sitting in a meeting room all day. They're used to dealing with problems and making rapid decisions. Training in small doses was minimally accepted. I knew my approach had to be engaging or I would lose their interest.

Luckily for me, team members had a willingness to learn and a good sense of humor. I infused the training with activities and things kept moving through the long first day. Everyone stayed engaged. When training was complete in the late afternoon, we walked to the line to see how Lean thinking could help us identify improvement opportunities.

There were many observations and ideas. The dirty condition of the equipment and floor, due to paint, grease, and fiberglass fibers was a safety opportunity. With no obvious tools to help the operators and mechanics do their jobs, I asked line operators what they did when repairs and adjustments were needed.

They showed me their personal tool boxes, which were in various stages of disarray. If they didn't have what was needed, they lost valuable time searching in other areas. Having the proper tools was a huge improvement opportunity. We completed the walk and the team went home.

The next morning, we shared ideas to improve the situation at the line. One theme rose above all others: *Provide the proper tools where needed, when needed, to improve the safety and productivity of the line.*

This meant tools would have to be taken out of tool boxes and arranged visibly, where they could be accessed by anyone at any time. When the team prioritized projects to work on, *tool availability and visibility* was at the bottom of the list.

There was something they weren't telling me. Upon further discussion, trust was revealed to be the reason *tool availability and visibility* wasn't prioritized higher. Team members felt their co-workers couldn't be trusted to return tools when they were finished using them. Even worse, they thought contractors intentionally took tools out of the plant. I had to suggest something extreme to overcome the trust issues and refocus efforts on solving this critical problem.

"Paint them **PINK!**" They looked at me as if I were from Mars. "Let me explain. If you paint all tools pink and hang them on a board, no one will wonder where they came from, lose them, or take them out of the plant. Who wants a pink wrench?" Now they were laughing. I wasn't kidding. I wanted to demonstrate there was an answer and nothing should stand in the way of doing the right thing. Team members discussed the merits of creating a board with pink tools. They weren't yet convinced this idea would work. At a break, I walked to Steve's office and poked my head inside.

Me: "Hey Steve, sorry to interrupt, but I need to discuss something critical with you. Do you have some time for me?"

Steve: "Sure thing Adam, what's up?"

Me: "We're trying to figure out how to make tools available to everyone on the line, without locking them in tool boxes. The team is having trouble with trust. They're afraid tools will be lost or walk out of the plant if they make them visible and available for everyone to use."

Steve: "I've heard the stories of tools being taken out of the plant. We think it may be some of our contractors."

Me: "I've been pushing the team to create a system where no tools can be lost. It'll save valuable time and improve safety. They're not buying it at the moment."

Steve: "Sounds challenging. What can I do to help?"

This was my opportunity to coach Steve around his leadership support for the team.

Me: "The team is going to do their best to develop a system to ensure tools never leave the factory and are always available to those who need them. But, they're new at this. Rules will be broken. They need your leadership when that happens."

Steve: "I'm almost afraid to ask. What do you suggest?"

Me: "At the report out, they're going to introduce the rule: *Tools are either in use or on the tool board. Nowhere else, **EVER.***"

Steve: "Seems like the right thing to do. I can reinforce the rule at the report out and in crew meetings."

Me: "That's great, but we're going to need more than that. Someone is going to break the rule. The first time that happens, we need you to pound your fist and stomp your feet. Make such a fuss everyone will remember it."

Steve: "Seriously? You want me to pound my fist and stomp my feet?"

Me: "How often have you done anything like that?"

Steve: "Well, never. It's not my style. You know that."

Me: "Do it once. I'm certain you'll never need to do it again."

Steve: "That seems a little extreme, even for you. I know you think you're doing what's right. Let me think about it."

Me: "Hey, thanks for listening. We're counting on you."

I left Steve's office and returned to the meeting room. The team decided to build a tool board and sent me to the hardware store to get red (not *pink*) paint and other supplies. When I returned, some team members filled the board with tools they painted red. Other team members organized and cleaned the rest of the line. It was an amazing transformation. You could sense the safety and productivity improving.

At the report out, the team pleaded for help to maintain the conditions of the line and keep the tools on the new board. Steve chimed in to reinforce the importance of the new rule: *Tools are either in use or on the tool board. Nowhere else,* **EVER**. After much congratulating, the team disbanded, their job well done.

Two months later, I was facilitating another Kaizen team at the plant. During our Gemba walk, I was called over by an operator from the original 5S team. He showed me the tool board with all tools in their proper places. I asked him if anyone tried to break the rule. He said it happened two weeks after the Kaizen event. When Steve heard about it, he raised such a fuss it shocked everyone. Best of all, it never happened again.

It's Better to be Red than Green

We've been taught Red means "*Stop*" and Green means "*Go*". In the context of process improvement, Red means something isn't performing as expected. Green means everything is okay. But is it okay?

Most people don't want to admit their process is Red. They think Red makes them look bad and will typically report things are Green. The problem is they're missing an opportunity to get help before a small problem becomes a big problem.

They go along thinking "*I got this, it's going to be okay,*" and report as Green, until "*uh oh, it's not going to be okay,*" and they need help to get things back on track. At this point, it may be too late, too difficult, or expensive to resolve their issues.

Encourage people to report Red and ask for help. It should be simple and non-threatening. On a benchmarking visit to an office furniture manufacturer, our tour guide told us, "We rally to the Red." I realized, at that moment, it was the right way to get people to self-report problems and request help.

Red is a call to action, a call for help. It's not a personal failure. It's everyone's priority to help get things back to Green. Imagine how much wasted effort and cost could be avoided if people exposed issues sooner and got help to resolve those issues.

Compare this to the manager, when told a project has Red status who says, *"what are you doing to get to Green?"* The burden is on the person who reported Red. Help doesn't seem forthcoming. The person who identified the issue probably thinks, *"I wish I hadn't brought it up. I won't make that mistake next time."*

Status Indicators

During a Kaizen event, teams identify projects to work on and then go off and do the work, hoping to return with a finished product. In my early experience, I allowed team members to work on their own. I hoped they would complete their work in a reasonable amount of time. It didn't always turn out that way. Hope is not a plan.

They rarely completed their work on time. More often, they lost time and progress because they got stuck and no one knew about it. I started to rotate through groups to assess progress. That relied on one person:

me. After a time, I realized there was a better way to track progress, make it visible, and create engagement. The answer: Status Indicators.

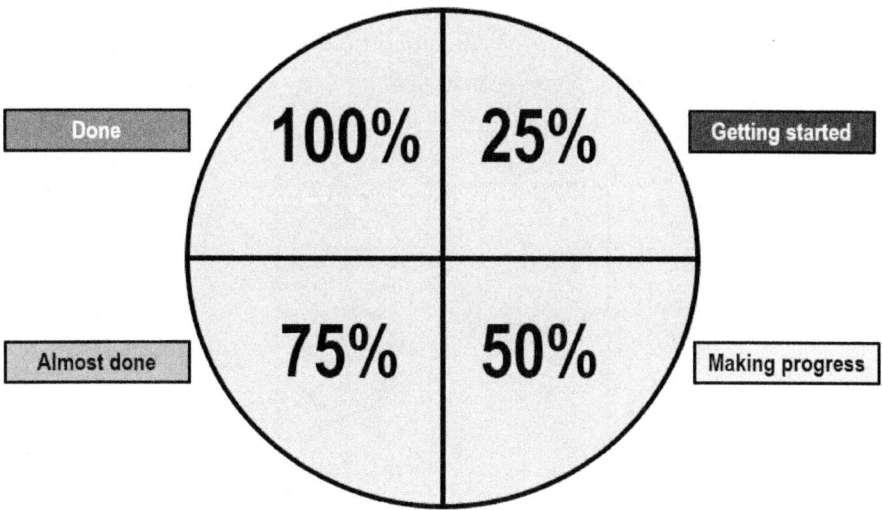

Here's how Status Indicators work:

Draw a circle. Break it into quadrants. Fill in each quadrant using a marker, indicating progress towards completion. It doesn't have to be scientific or pretty, it just has to work.

25% = **Getting started** – initial progress has been made or a plan has been created.

50% = **Making progress** – things are moving along and people know what to do and how to do it.

75% = **Almost there** – we can see the light at the end of the tunnel. We can finish the work.

100% = **Done** – we're finished and ready to move on to something else.

There's no need to break status down into smaller elements. That would cause the team to spend more time updating status and less time doing work. When properly updated, it's powerful and simple to understand. I use flip chart paper to draw Status Indicators during Kaizen events. Flip chart paper is large enough to allow others to see status from twenty feet away or more.

To give you a sense for the value and impact of Status Indicators, use the following example. Four teams are working on separate projects. Their Status Indicators look like this:

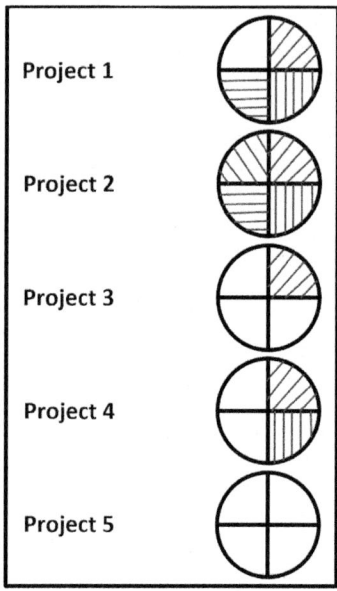

Project 1 is *Almost there*, Project 2 is *Done*, Project 3 is *Getting started*, Project 4 is *Making progress*, and Project 5 hasn't been started. It's clear who needs help and who can help. Team members from Project 2 can help Projects 3 and 4, depending on their skills and interests. If there are more resources than Projects 3 and 4 need, those resources can start on Project 5. Anyone else, even if they're not on the team, can assess status and help those who need it.

The value of Status Indicators has been reinforced to me many times, never more than when I forgot to use them. After a particularly busy day during a Kaizen event, some team members said they were frustrated because they didn't know what to do next. Others said the day felt chaotic and disorganized. I realized I hadn't trained the team to use Status

Indicators. I immediately showed them how to use them. The next day, much more work got completed. At the end of the day, the team related how much easier it was to manage their work.

From a supervisor's or manager's point of view, Status Indicators make it simpler and more efficient to keep track of work going on in many areas. Hours of effort to track progress are reduced to minutes or seconds.

Status Indicators are Visible Evidence. They can be used to reinforce critical efforts and sustain the changes being implemented. If you are tracking Training and Review across an organization, place a Status Indicator next to a picture of each person being trained. Ask them to update their training status. Audit and follow up to ensure they have everything they need to be successfully trained. If someone hasn't made sufficient progress, provide the time, resources, and help to reach the required level of competency.

A team I worked with created a Training Tracking board. Across the top of the board were pictures of twenty-four team members. Down the side were five critical training modules. There were Status Indicators at every intersection. That's 120 trainings to be tracked. It sounds like a lot to look at, but based on their design, the entire group could be assessed within minutes.

How to tell if someone is doing something in the right order

One of the key elements of Visible Evidence is to make sure the process, procedure, or instruction is being followed in the proper order. To assess this, you must be willing to watch and engage. But, how do you know proper order is being followed? There are choices: you can ask, you can compare movements to the documented procedure, or let Visible Evidence provide the answer. Some ways to accomplish this include:

- Create a visual showing each step pictorially. Show the area, location, and task to be performed prior to moving on to the next task.
- Put labels at each step to be performed and number them appropriately.

- Put step numbers in the location where the work is to be completed. This could be on a sign, a label on the floor, a label on equipment, or other means.
- If you want an example of an organization who does this very well, consider Disney World's approach to visually indicate the order of activities for visitors of all ages and languages.

Should visuals be automated?

I have had many discussions about the merits of automated versus manually updated visuals. There are valid arguments for either choice. My preference is to manually create and update visuals. My reasons:

1. Anyone can update a manual visual – it doesn't require training or security access.
2. When you update something manually, you get internal satisfaction. Think about list makers who put checkmarks next to their completed tasks. Each time they do, they feel a sense of accomplishment.
3. People are more inclined to engage with something they can personally interact with than something that's just a graphical display. I have seen people cross out numbers, draw pictures, and generally create on a white board or flip chart. It's difficult to do that with a computer screen.
4. Manual visuals aren't intimidating. People don't feel like they are being talked down to. Anyone can create a manual visual.
5. Manual visuals are easier and faster to create. There's no need to wait on a system or acquire programming skills.

Automated visuals have their merits. Newer systems are easier to use and encourage engagement. Choose manual, automated, or a combination. Be sure to apply the principles of Visible Evidence to whatever solution you choose.

Less than Success Story

Who Are We Designing This for?

I visited an engineered wood flooring plant in Kentucky. They were losing millions of dollars annually due to poor scrap performance. After meeting with the Plant Manager and his leadership team, we took a Gemba walk to assess the current situation.

The plant was fairly well organized and clean. Everyone was following the safety rules and were intent on keeping themselves safe. How did I know this? I saw Visible Evidence of the Leadership Commitment to safety. There was signage that was aligned with actions of the leaders and all employees.

I noticed a huge amount of scrap materials in the plant. Pallets of flooring boards were lying around and it seemed like more scrap was being made by the minute. I asked how production and scrap information was tracked and was directed to a large white board mounted to the outer wall of an office.

The board displayed information on the products being produced and the hourly output of the various production lines. There was no display of scrap or quality information. I wanted to understand how the board was used. I asked the team to wait by the board until someone interacted with it.

Ten minutes later, a production operator walked up to the board with paper in her hand. She looked rushed and stressed. She left her line while it was running, walked twenty yards, and transferred information from the paper to the board. She acknowledged us and then rushed back to her line.

As we walked around the rest of the factory, I noticed there were no production boards at any of the lines. Everyone had to walk away from what they were doing and go to the main production board to enter information on an hourly basis. Sometimes, they were so busy they didn't update information. The leadership team lamented that fact and wondered what could be done about it.

I shared these suggestions with the team:

- Place the information in a convenient spot to the person who maintains and uses it.
- Train the leadership team to go to the information, rather than making it come to them.
- Engage with the person doing the work in their own space and in their own time.

The team was intrigued and thought it might be helpful to incorporate these ideas and other principles of Visible Evidence into a Kaizen event designed to improve quality and scrap performance. A month later we kicked off the Kaizen. The rest of the story, "*350 Employees Became 350 Business Owners*," can be found in Chapter 10.

Visible Evidence at Home

Do you ever lose or misplace tools? I used to. I was tired of trying to find what I needed and going up and down stairs to chase down the tools I used to do work in my garage and outside. One day, I decided to do something about it. I identified what I was bringing up from my basement. I also had some garden tools lying on shelves that were hidden and hard to find.

Using a clear spot on the garage wall, I attached the largest pegboard that would fit. I identified the tools I used the most and hung them up on the board. If there was something I had to buy, such as a set of screw drivers, I went to the store. It's always fun to buy new tools. The board has a combination of garage and garden tools on it.

Although the tools aren't outlined and labeled, I'm able to quickly tell if anything's missing. If a hook doesn't have a tool on it, it's missing. In my house, it can't have gone far. Driving into my garage, I'm able to assess status of all tools on the board. That's my audit. I know my system is working every day.

Another example of Visible Evidence can be found in our kitchen pantry. Peggy has plastic containers labeled with contents and expiration dates. She uses large, easy to read labels. We can quickly and easily identify contents and be assured everything is fresh. It makes shopping and meal planning simple and effective. Nothing gets lost and we constantly rotate our inventory.

How to Develop Effective Visible Evidence

Create a clear message

What is the message the visual is trying to portray? Stick to the main message. Use pictures, graphics, and as few words as possible.

Make it impossible to do the wrong thing

Have you made the visual so easy to follow that there's no way to do work incorrectly? Can anyone discern if things are correct or incorrect?

Keep it simple

Convey the message in as simple a way as possible. Don't put too much information in one visual. The message should be understood in less than five seconds of study.

Visuals are reinforcing, not distracting

Is the visual reinforcing the right way to do the work? Can it be placed in a location that's easy to see but not in the way? Pay attention to the overall system to optimize placement.

Put the visual where the work is done

Put the message right where it's needed. Don't hide it. Duplicate it if there are multiple locations where it needs to be shared. People tend to forget things. Repetition is encouraged.

Size matters

Make visuals as large as possible. Be careful not to make them so big they distract or get in the way of doing the job or block the sight line of the person using them.

Eliminate the need to refer to something else

Visuals should be self-explanatory. If you have to refer to something else, there is more chance to forget a critical detail or make an error.

Survival of the fittest

Visuals must survive in the environment where they're displayed. Paper gets damaged easily. If you must use it, laminate it. If the visual needs to stay in a location, adhere it to a surface or chain it in place. Don't put it far away from the area where it will be used.

Be creative

Use any surface to create Visible Evidence. Floors, cabinets, walls, boards, and equipment can be used. The more creative you are, the more likely people will notice.

Effective visuals

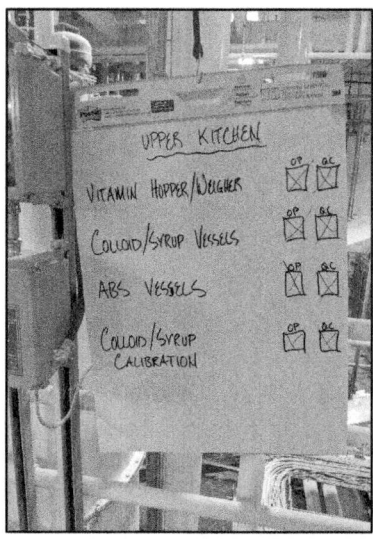

Placed near the critical bracket. Picture and words show exactly what to do.	Large size, easy to read, and indicates everyone has finished their tasks.

Mistakes to Avoid

Using incomplete or unclear visuals

Assuming pre-existing knowledge or skill mastery isn't helpful or practical. There are many different people who rely on the visuals. Not everyone has the same level of understanding.

Requiring reference to another document or visual

People are unlikely to track down the next piece of information if it's not right where they need it, when they need it. They're likely to work from memory and make a mistake or overlook a step.

Using one location or an inconvenient location

People have short attention spans. If you think they'll remember what they're supposed to do when they're away from the information, you're fooling yourself.

Insulting or demeaning messages

We deserve to be treated with respect. If you wouldn't say it to someone you care about, don't put it on a visual. Humor is fine, but be careful. Someone could be offended.

Sending contradictory messages

If you aren't willing to do something, don't expect someone else to.

Ineffective visuals

Is this really what you want employees to see every time they use the time clock?	Who's responsible to clean up their mess? Does anyone believe this will happen?

How Leadership Commitment Supports Visible Evidence

Visible Evidence is used to help people do the right thing at all times. It identifies when people aren't working to standard. Leaders should be looking for Visible Evidence in their daily routines. If they don't see indications people are doing the right things, they must engage immediately and offer help. They assess the Visible Evidence to ascertain if it's aligned with the messages they are sending. If it needs to be improved, they deliver feedback to the team who created the visuals.

Leaders offer help in a positive way. They shouldn't accept deviations from the standard without engaging. Put the burden on the system, not the person. If the visuals aren't understood, take the time to explain their meaning.

Don't worry about having too many signs. Provide signs to help people do the right thing. Support the visuals and keep testing them for alignment with the message to be conveyed.

Summary

Visible Evidence helps anyone in the organization assess the status and health of the operating system. The goal is to provide status from twenty feet away or more. Simple visuals make the system easy to train and understand. Design visuals in a way that they're easy to find, see, and reinforce the changes.

Once you have created Visible Evidence and verify it supports the changes, it's time to move on to the next spoke on the Wheel of Sustainability, All Tools Available.

Visible Evidence Takeaways:

How strong Leadership Commitment supports Visible Evidence:

How weak Leadership Commitment damages Visible Evidence:

What I can do to improve my approach to Visible Evidence:

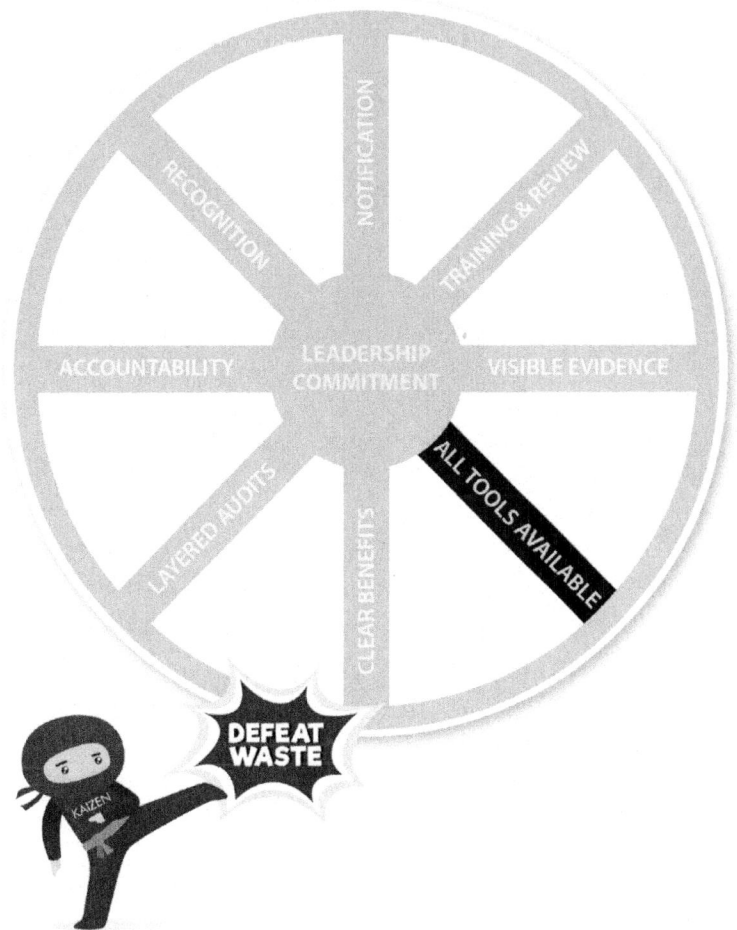

ALL TOOLS AVAILABLE

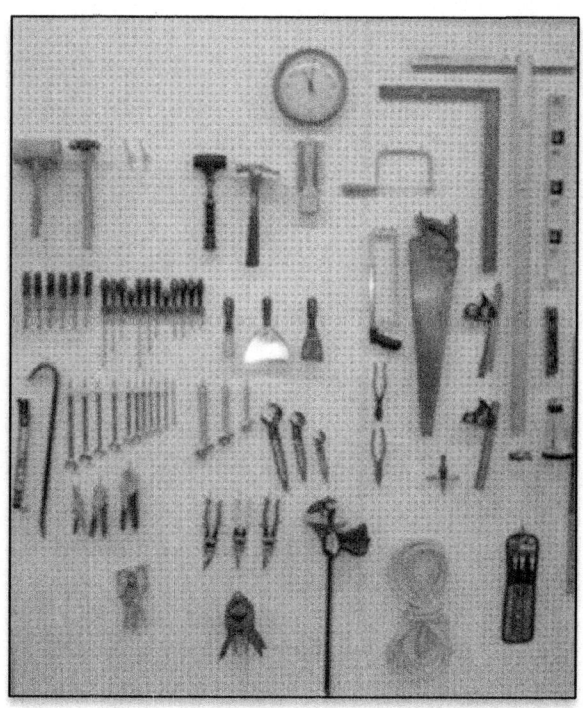

All Tools Available provides everything necessary to accomplish work in the safest, lowest stress, and most productive way.

Introduction

There was a commercial many years ago that showed employees sitting around a table trying to solve a problem. They only had one pen. When someone needed to write, they had to borrow it from the person using it. Their frustration was palpable.

The commercial was funny and creative. It showed what happens when you don't give people what they need to work safely and effectively. It illustrates the need for the fourth spoke on the Wheel of Sustainability, All Tools Available. This spoke ensures everyone can properly follow the changes by giving them what they need.

Everything needed to accomplish work is provided to the person doing the work in a convenient location. There's no need to transport tools. They're waiting for you where you need them. If there are multiple locations, tools are duplicated and positioned locally. In a factory setting, this eliminates the need to carry tools with you, store them in a tool box, or search for them. All Tools Available reduces time, effort, and safety risk.

In an office setting, you are able to find the supplies you need where and when you need them. You don't have to search or wait for them to be replenished. Your computer has the capacity, programs, apps, and flexibility required. You don't have to borrow a travel laptop to work from home or wait for IT to install a critical program. You have the ability to work remotely without fear of security lapses or insufficient bandwidth.

People worry they'll have to spend a lot of money to implement All Tools Available. It turns out it doesn't have to be expensive. Only critical tools and supplies are defined and provided in the quantities required. The value of having tools where you need them and when you need them outweighs the cost of the extras. If you avoid duplication, it will cost you more in time, effort, and risk.

This may sound counter to the Lean principle of *"inventory is waste"*. This isn't inventory. It's what's needed to do your job safely and productively. If you use 5S to determine the tools critical for the job, you'll reduce excess tools by 50 percent or more.

How 5S Supports All Tools Available

In Chapter 4, I reviewed the 5S approach to creating Visible Evidence for the tools, systems, procedures, and other things to make it easy to tell if things are going well or poorly. 5S also supports All Tools Available. Here's how it works:

Sort

Sort eliminates clutter. Identify what is critical and necessary and remove everything else. We have now identified the critical tools needed.

Set in Order

Tools are arranged in such a way that they are easy to find, cannot be lost, and are safe to use. Safety and productivity are optimized for the user of the tools. Identify multiple locations, if necessary, for critical tools.

Shine

Critical tools are maintained in optimal condition. They work any time and every time. There is low risk of failure. If a tool is in need of repair when performing Shine, it is repaired or replaced immediately.

Standardize

Create audits to ensure tools aren't lost and conditions stay optimal. The organization supports the efforts of the team who uses the tools to do their work. Standardize reinforces the importance of the system to respect the tools through the auditing process.

Sustain

Sustain challenges the organization to continually improve the system. Do we have the proper tools? Are they optimally placed? Are there other tools, documents, or visuals to improve the safety and productivity of the area?

Principles of All Tools Available

- Everything required to do work is provided, logically located, and is easy to find.
- There's no need to transport tools to locations where they're needed. They're already there.
- Duplication of critical tools is accepted and encouraged.

Success Stories

This Stuff Works

At a gummy vitamin manufacturer in Pennsylvania, I was engaged to facilitate a team of mechanics responsible for supporting and maintaining the manufacturing operations. They had difficulty keeping their area compliant with strict food production regulations. Our goal was to develop a system to guarantee compliance, while improving their ability to service their customers.

The first thing we did was review Lean principles and how 5S is used to optimize safety and productivity. It all sounds good in a classroom. The team wasn't sure it applied to them. They thought they were in pretty good shape. We took a Gemba walk through their work space and performed a 5S audit.

The space was cluttered and lacked any hint of organization. They had nothing to compare to and hadn't been exposed to other examples of 5S. We scored the area at 0.8 out of 5 possible points. They were shocked. After generating improvement ideas, we walked to two locations in the plant that had implemented 5S.

Our first stop was a production line. I asked a technician to give the team a 5S tour. He obliged and described 5S and its benefits from his point of view. Team members paid attention, but asked few questions and wrote fewer notes. We thanked him and walked to the Weld shop.

On the way, I asked team members what they thought of 5S on the production line. Feedback fell into two categories:

1. It looks pretty good.
2. We don't see how it applies to us.

I was sure the next tour stop would be more inspiring. Intimately familiar with what was done in the area, I could provide a more compelling review for the team.

When we entered the Weld shop, I noticed Sammy working on a project. He was the team leader from an earlier 5S Kaizen event. His story can be found in Chapter 7 (*Owning Their Solution in the Weld Shop*).

Sammy: "What are you doing here? Can't you see I'm busy?"

Me: "Sorry for the interruption Sammy. This is the 5S Kaizen team. I'm giving them a tour to show them what your team accomplished."

Sammy: "Okay, just don't get in the way. I've got lots of work to do."

Me: "Thanks. If you want to share your thoughts on 5S, please do."

Sammy: "No thanks. You can give the tour."

Sammy isn't someone who likes to speak in front of groups or work with teams. He's not a fan of management or consultants. He doesn't give out compliments and doesn't fall in line and just do whatever he's told. If he believes in something that aligns with management, that gets people's attention.

I began by pointing out various improvements the Weld shop Kaizen team made six months earlier. Sammy paid attention, but didn't say a word. I think he was interested to hear my description of the work of his team. I did my best to represent their efforts. The pride showed in Sammy's face.

My next stop on the tour was at a tool board created during the Kaizen event. As I described and demonstrated the use of the tool board, Sammy got more interested. Team members were asking questions and taking notes.

Rob (team leader): "This looks good and all. Does it really stay this way?"

Me: "They didn't clean things up just because we were coming to see them."

Ben (team member): "This doesn't seem real. Everything looks like it's in a museum. Does it really work?"

Sammy: "Look, this may sound silly and it may sound stupid. ***THIS $#*% WORKS!***"

This was the moment of clarity and credibility for the team. If Sammy thought so, it must be so. The tour was over. The team had seen everything they needed.

I thanked Sammy. We walked back to the meeting room to review observations and ideas. On the way, I challenged team members to beat the results of the production line and the Weld shop. They told me they were up for the challenge.

The rest of the week, the team identified the critical tools and duplicated them where necessary (All Tools Available), gave them visible and logical homes (Visible Evidence), and told the leadership team what they needed from them to sustain the efforts (Layered Audits and Accountability). They scored their newly organized area 4.7 out of 5. Quite an improvement from the 0.8 baseline. I'm not sure their area was any better than the other 5S areas, but they thought so, and that's all that matters.

From Tool Boxes to Tool Stations

I flew to Florida to facilitate a changeover reduction Kaizen at a ceiling tile plant. Most changeover reduction events have a goal of reducing time by 50 percent, while maintaining or improving safety and quality. The team was asked to reduce changeover time on the edge finishing line by 90 percent. I wondered if we could achieve this challenging goal.

Ceiling tile edges were cut and painted before being sent to the packaging line. Using a panel saw called an equalizer, tiles were cut to a rough size. Four machines (tenoners) cut and painted the edges of the tiles to achieve precise outer dimensions and edge finish. The tiles were designed to fit snugly into ceiling grid. A portion of the tile hung below the surface of the grid, creating a three-dimensional look.

The tenoners had dozens of adjustment points, requiring wrenches and other tools to meet strict dimensional tolerances. All technicians had personal tool boxes, which they stored away from the line. When it was time to adjust or set up the tenoners, they gathered tools and carried them to the tenoner they were adjusting at the moment.

After reviewing Lean principles and Single Minute Exchange of Die (SMED), we observed a changeover conducted by the crew on shift. There

THE WHEEL OF SUSTAINABILITY | 117

was a tremendous amount of walking, due to gathering and moving tools back and forth between the equipment and tool boxes.

After ninety minutes, the changeover was complete. Therefore, our goal was to achieve a consistent nine-minute changeover. There appeared to be a tremendous amount of opportunity to reduce all of the walking. Would it be enough to achieve our goal?

SMED

Single Minute Exchange of Die. Used to reduce changeover time using a four-step method. Originally developed by Shigeo Shingo for Toyota in the 1960s, it is used by companies all around the world. Watch a pit stop during an auto race to see how it works.

After brainstorming improvement ideas, I asked the team to focus on ways to eliminate the huge amount of walking we observed. The plant was built in the 1940s. Habits were developed over decades of production. I hoped people would be willing to give up their personal tool boxes.

They weren't willing to, but it didn't matter. The team decided tool boxes should be kept for unscheduled repairs and adjustments. Placing changeover-specific tools right at the place they were needed would save a huge amount of time.

We identified three tools used to set the saws and edge paint sprayers. They were needed in eight separate locations. Were we willing to replicate those three tools eight times?

If we wanted to reduce the time by 90 percent, we had to be willing to take extreme measures. I was sent to the hardware store to buy what we needed. The team mounted the tools in ideal locations for changeover adjustments.

We created visuals to illustrate changeover steps and installed a large digital clock on a post. It displayed the elapsed changeover time. We tested our new procedure and were able to complete the changeover in 15 minutes by the end of the Kaizen event.

Although we didn't meet our goal, changeover time was reduced by 83 percent. The team felt they had won and the plant reaped the benefits of a safer and quicker changeover for many years thereafter.

Four Value Streams = Four Boards

I reported to George, the Vice President of Global Technology, for a ceiling tile company. We kicked off our Lean transformation and established four Value Streams: Innovation (R&D), New Product Development, Capital Engineering, and Business and Operations Support. Value Stream Directors guided efforts to deliver value to the internal and external customers who relied on their critical results.

While the Value Streams had different customers to serve and missions to accomplish, they interacted frequently and shared resources. I supported all Value Streams and had the opportunity to build relationships across many areas of the business. We aligned around the need to keep critical information in front of us and engage with it at all times.

We agreed to use white boards to display the most relevant and critical information for everyone to see and act on. During Value Stream huddles, the boards would be reviewed for decisions to be made and documented. Some of the teams took this need for a white board to be a requirement. They put together their boards and huddles just because they thought George and Adam said it must be done.

It quickly became apparent the boards weren't helping the teams accomplish work more productively or safely than before they were established. One team got rebellious and made their huddle a grind, rather than a value-adding exercise. Snide remarks and rushing through information replaced deep discussion and problem solving.

George and I called a meeting with the four Value Stream Directors. We drew out the reasons for their resistance. They thought the boards were prescriptive, leaving no room to design for the purpose of their individual Value Streams. They thought everything had to look and act the same, even if it didn't work.

Once the problem was revealed, we were ready to improve the situation. We declared that design of the boards and huddles should be left to the Value Stream teams. They'd decide what was most relevant and useful and design their boards and huddles accordingly.

I offered to help the teams redesign their new boards and huddles. Two teams accepted my offer. The others did it on their own. We agreed to use these design principles:

- Boards and huddles have the tools and information to help the team make decisions simply and quickly.
- It doesn't matter what the board looks like. If it helps, that's all that matters.
- Make problems and requests for help visible.
- Design the board for the use of the Value Stream team. We'll teach the leaders how to read the boards and provide support.

All teams redesigned their boards and huddles within a month. None of the boards looked alike. Over the next months and years, they redesigned and improved their boards and huddles many times. The information became more relevant, urgent, and beneficial to their employees, their customers, and the Global Technology group.

We were benchmarked by many other groups due to our impressive results. Many asked why the boards weren't standardized, allowing anyone to read and understand any of them without training.

We explained that the teams came first. They were working on what was right for the business and the boards helped them do just that. We taught our leaders how to read the boards and support the teams. Those who challenged our thinking didn't always like the answer. We knew we were giving our employees all the tools they needed to make the best possible decisions for themselves, their customers, and the business.

Less than Success Story

Saving Is Not Saving

We were building a ceiling tile manufacturing plant in Russia. Like most projects, the engineering team was directed to save money, as long as it didn't negatively impact safety or productivity. As most were unfamiliar with doing business in Russia, they used their experience with known vendors to acquire equipment for the plant. If there wasn't enough capacity to fill equipment needs, the project team worked with local consultants to identify the "*best*" options for equipment purchases.

A few years earlier we had shuttered a plant in Alabama. Equipment was stored in the hopes it might be used for future projects. The project team identified equipment they thought they could use and had it shipped to a contractor, who was responsible to inspect it and bring it up to optimal operating condition. This was done to save more than $1 million for the project.

Two weeks before plant start-up, I traveled to Russia to assess and optimize the flow of ceiling tiles through the new production line. I had done this work many times in other manufacturing plants and was known as the flow "*expert*".

When I arrived, I was assigned a team of two mechanics and one production operator. We were going to send ceiling tiles through various parts of the line and make adjustments and corrections where necessary to improve the flow.

Very few tools were available for our use. I packed string, levels, and flat steel bars to help us with the work. Our initial assessment and work through the line went smoothly. We identified conveyers that were out of level, causing the ceiling tiles to skew and jam. Fixing these problems was simple enough. Soon we had tiles flowing smoothly through the first half of the line. Until we reached the equalizer.

The equalizer is a large panel saw. Its purpose is to cut ceiling boards into finished ceiling tiles. The board goes through a first set of saws, strikes a transfer, and then is driven through a second set of saws positioned at a right angle.

Boards were going through the saws at an angle. Instead of tiles looking like rectangles, they looked like trapezoids. They weren't going to fit into ceiling grid that way.

There were many possible reasons for the angled cuts. After resolving many issues, the tiles still weren't correct. What was going on? Normally, fixes happen independently of the saw assemblies. Saws are typically located in a level and square way on a frame. Everything else controls how the boards come to the saws in a square or angled fashion.

In this case, the problem was in the saw assembly. We locked out and climbed up on the equipment to take a closer look. The equalizer was freshly painted and made to look as if it was new. But it was far from new. There were many missing or broken parts. Because of that, we couldn't control the boards as they were being cut. Broken motor mounts caused the saw blades to rotate in an elliptical fashion. How did the contractor miss this critical detail? How did we miss this during equipment inspection?

We spent the rest of our time repairing or replacing broken parts. Some things couldn't be fixed immediately. We ordered parts and equipment from other locations. Some had to be air-freighted from the United States at considerable cost. All fixes were completed prior to the official plant start-up, but took valuable resources away from other critical work. All of this could have been avoided had the project team recognized the critical influence of the equalizer and chosen to invest in the right tools for the new plant. Expected savings disappeared due to the lack of All Tools Available.

All Tools Available at Home or in the Office

How to Apply All Tools Available to Your Computer or Mobile Device

We live in a world where we're constantly inundated with new and more powerful apps, tools, and programs for our mobile devices and computers. As soon as you get comfortable using an app, another one comes along with the promise of a better experience.

Most of us use less than 10 percent of the capability of any app, computer program, or hardware. Updates sound nice, but don't impact productivity for the typical user. I recommend you identify the features needed to make you productive. Once you do, commit to them. Resist the urge to upgrade to the newest version.

Screen out all of the noise of *"new and better"* and become comfortable with what you have. Once you make this commitment, you'll find out you don't need as many devices, programs, hardware, apps, etc. From here on, I'll use the term *"stuff"*.

With less *stuff*, determine the best placement and organization to maximize your productivity. Don't skimp on what you need to do your job. You don't have to have the best of everything. But, if you want, you can treat yourself to some *stuff* to future-proof your situation.

If you're not a gamer, chances are you don't need the top-of-the-line processor. You may want it anyway, to be a few seconds faster when your computer boots up or runs complex programs. I always underestimate the amount of storage required. If you need additional storage, use the cloud. It may keep you from investing in more expensive equipment.

Next, consider how to find your *stuff*. Limit the quantity by deciding on what you need and committing to it. On your mobile device, you may have one hundred apps instead of three hundred. On your computer, you may have twenty critical programs instead of fifty. Identify those programs and apps and place them in the most obvious, easy to access locations.

Place highest priority apps on the home screen of your mobile device. All other apps should be placed on the next screens. Using this approach, you're reminded what's most important every time you turn on your mobile device.

On your computer, place the twenty critical programs, apps, or folders on your desktop. Put nothing else there. Arrange them in priority order. Follow the principle of putting things where they are needed. Use the task bar for the highest of the high priority programs and apps. You now have Visible Evidence of your tools in multiple places.

File Arrangement

I don't purge my computer files often. It's easy for critical files to get lost. I use a system for arranging files in priority order. It helps me find what I need easily. This example is on a Windows computer, and is applicable to Apple products as well. Using the Documents folder as a starting place (or My Documents for users with older computers), I use this structure:

Documents
      01–**Project Files** of Highest Priority
          01–**Sub-Project Files** of Highest Priority within the
Project File
          02–**Sub-Project Files** of Second Highest Priority within
the Project File
      02–**Project Files** of Second Highest Priority
      03–**Project Files** of Third Highest Priority
      :
      :

      99–**Project Files** of Ninety-Ninth Highest Priority

My files currently look like this (client names omitted):

Documents
      01–Business Related Information
      02–Content
          01–Blogs
          02–Videos
          03–Podcasts
          04–Standard Work Files
      03–Client #1
          01–Location #1
          02–Location #2
      04–Client #2
      05–Client #3
      :
      :
      09–Client #7
      10–Historical Files
      11–Personal Files
      12–Miscellaneous Files

This structure allows me to see my most important files first. The computer sorts files alpha-numerically. The lowest number always is at the top of the screen. I reevaluate priorities quarterly. An inactive client may be at the top of the list. When that happens, I rename and reprioritize my folders. I only need to change the numbers.

For example, let's say Client #2 becomes inactive. Folder "04–Client #2" is renamed "13–Client #2". The folder is now at the bottom of the list. I then make a decision. Do I renumber the other folders or just wait for a new client to emerge? If I leave things alone, the name change takes seconds.

Although there is a search function on the computer, I still find this file structure saves me time. I don't suggest that you use this system, unless you think it will help you. If you've ever asked yourself: "Where is that file," this structure all but eliminates searching. I now have All Tools Available on my computer.

All Tools Available in the Office

Tools in the office include computers, printers, furniture, pens, and other items. Have we provided office workers the tools they need to do their jobs safely and productively? Do they find themselves waiting for someone to finish with equipment or supplies before they can use them? If so, you haven't provided All Tools Available.

My son works for a call center. The first two years of his career, he wasn't able to take calls from home and had to go to the office to do his job. Some co-workers were able to take calls from their homes using company-supplied laptops. It didn't seem fair to me. The company wasn't supporting everyone with All Tools Available.

As an experiment, the company let him borrow a laptop, a payment device, and other accessories to work from home. On his first day, he figured out where to work (my hobby room), how to work (his new routine), and when and how to take breaks. He soon realized what he had been missing.

His company has since outfitted everyone to work from home, spending the money required to give them what they need to do their job safely and productively.

Working from home reduces the cost to the company and increases flexibility for its employees. There have been times my son chose to work on a day he wasn't feeling well. Had he been required to go to the office, he would have taken a sick day. Providing All Tools Available has benefited the company, its employees, and by extension, its customers.

Ergonomic Workstation Setup

Many of us work from home. It's best to use ergonomic principles for workstation setup. When followed, you'll be safer and more productive. If not, you may find yourself suffering from eyestrain or sore muscles at the end of the day. There's much research and documentation about ergonomics. I will focus on how ergonomics should be applied using the principles of All Tools Available.

The most important tools are your muscles. You don't have extras. You need to treat them as tenderly as possible. They should be relaxed and in a neutral position, which reduces stress on them. Here's how[3]:

- **Wrists** – Keep the line between your forearm and hand straight.
- **Elbows** – Maintain a 90- to 110-degree angle between your forearm and biceps.
- **Feet** – Flat on the floor or on a foot rest.
- **Knees** – Maintain a 90- to 110-degree angle when seated. If standing, keep your knees slightly bent.
- **Eyes and neck** – Computer monitors should be positioned to comfortably look straight ahead or slightly down, not up. Draw a line from your eyes to the top edge of the monitor. If it's parallel to the floor, that's the ideal monitor height.
- **Standing** – Put tools and equipment at a height where muscles stay in neutral and strain is reduced. Waist height is ideal, typically between 36 and 42 inches off the floor.

---

[3] 3M Office Ergonomics Checklist – Document 34-8500-7437-7. http://www-ehs.ucsd.edu/ergo/pdf/ergochecklist.pdf

Other advice

- Don't skimp on tools you use to accomplish your work. Your chair needs to be comfortable. Your desk should be a desk.
- Place tools, equipment, and critical supplies within arm's reach. You won't lose time searching for things, unless you have a bunch of clutter. Look at the next piece of advice.

Put only *critical* materials, supplies, and tools out for use. Remove all clutter.

All Tools Available for Kaizen Events

I've facilitated hundreds of Kaizen events. I'm always looking for the easiest, most efficient way to prepare sponsors, leaders, and teams for a winning experience. One of the ways I have learned is to identify the tools required and make this part of the effort almost automatic.

These are All Tools Available for Kaizen events:

- **Charter** – The contract between the facilitator, sponsor, team leader, and ultimately, the team. It contains the problem to be solved, the Kaizen objectives, the team to engage, and the owner of the output. More information can be found in Chapter 10 (Leadership Commitment)
- **Meeting space** – Where will the team do its work? Is there enough room and wall space for brainstorming, prioritization, movement, and comfort of the team members? If the meeting space is virtual, make sure technology is available and easy to use for the team to do their work.
- **Food** – All teams must be fed (even virtual ones). I have facilitated teams responsible for bringing their own food. It hurt their feelings and reduced the positive energy of the Kaizen event. Feed your teams.
- **Screen and system to project information** – Consider how training and other information will be delivered. If you don't favor

PowerPoint or computer-generated training, use other means, such as games, simulations, flip charts, Training and Review, etc.

- **Flip chart easels and flip chart paper** – Used by the team and facilitator. Big paper holds big ideas. Write as large as you can, so everyone can see it from wherever they are sitting.
- **Post-it notes** – I favor 4" X 6". They're large enough to write ideas that can be read from a distance.
- **Fine point Sharpie pens** – Forces the team to write the right amount of information on a Post-it note without too much detail and in a way that it can be seen from a distance.
- **Flip chart markers** – Dedicated to the flip charts. Use multiple colors to draw attention.
- **Painter's tape or masking tape** – Ensures anything taped to a wall doesn't peel off paint, keeping the facilitator out of trouble.
- **Time** – Provide adequate focused time for training, work, and breaks.
- **Other items** – This depends on the type of Kaizen event and needs of the team. Examples include: clipboards, stop watches, camera, Smart Sheets, and supplies for interactive games and demonstrations.

How to Develop Effective All Tools Available

Identify tools required

What do you need to do work safely and effectively? Break the work down to its essence and identify the tools needed to accomplish the job. Design for the normal state of the work. Don't identify tools for every situation. Keep clutter to a minimum. Any additional tools can either be purchased later or stored in a different location, for *"just in case"* situations.

When to duplicate tools

- Multiple locations may need the same tools to be used at the same time.

- Work areas requiring the same tools aren't close to each other.
- Tools are difficult to transport, easily misplaced, or lost.
- Tools must be carried to a second location on the same piece of equipment that isn't easy to see.

As an example, an operator used a heavy wrench to remove bolts on both sides of a punch press. Instead of using the wrench on one side of the press and carrying it to the other side, the team bought a duplicate. They mounted the wrenches on both sides of the press. They were labeled "*North Side Punch Press Wrench*" and "*South Side Punch Press Wrench.*"

Tool placement

Eliminate searching for tools. Place at eye level and within arm's reach of the person using them in the area they're used. You may have to be creative to get as close to ideal as possible. Signage helps people find the tools they need, but it's no substitute for having the tools you need right in front of you. Use Visible Evidence principles. Make it easy for anyone to tell the tools are where they are supposed to be and everything is either working properly or someone needs help to get back to standard.

In the previous example, the North and South Punch Press wrenches were hung on hooks on tool boards located less than ten feet from the press. There was an outline for each wrench, with corresponding labeling above the outline. Boards were labeled, "*South Side Punch Press Tool Board*" and "*North Side Punch Press Tool Board.*"

How to make sure tools aren't misplaced or lost

People decide what to do with the tools they use. Some are more careful than others. Less careful users put down tools and forget where they put them. Using Visible Evidence, make it almost impossible to lose tools.

Use this rule: "*Tools are in use or in place. Nothing else is acceptable.*" Leaders must support and demonstrate their commitment to it. In Chapter 4, I shared the story of the *Pink Tools*. It demonstrated Leadership Commitment to supporting the team's efforts to keep tools in the plant. Tools were never lost again.

Create ownership for the tools

We've identified the tools needed to help people work safely and effectively. Everyone should respect the tools provided and understand and follow all the proper protocols. But life isn't so simple. Designate an *Area Owner* to manage use of the tools. Support the *Area Owner* if someone doesn't follow the *Rules of the Tools*.

Once you have identified an Area Owner, publicize it. Use Visible Evidence to accomplish this. Use a photo of the Area Owner, add contact details, and share expectations for the area. The message should fit the culture of your organization. This is an example:

Weld Shop
Joe the Caveman
800-GOTCAVE

This is my area.
I do everything I can to make it safe and productive for you.
Please do your best to keep it that way.

Mistakes to Avoid

Not giving people what they need where they need it

If there are three locations that use the same tool, you may be tempted to just buy one tool and require people to carry it from place to place. The risk is it will be put down in one location and forgotten until it's needed in another location. Valuable time will be lost.

Not maintaining tools in optimal condition

It's really frustrating when you are trying to use something that doesn't work as it should. You'll lose time, become stressed, and may be exposed to safety risk. Would you use a ladder with a broken rung to climb to a high elevation? Of course not.

Using the wrong tool for the job

Have you ever seen someone use a wrench as a hammer? Many have done this, due to circumstances, convenience, or lack of patience. If you don't give people what they need, they'll use what they have. Don't give people the opportunity to do the wrong thing.

Buying cheap tools to save money

Using cheap tools puts your safety and productivity at risk. You can buy a screwdriver for less than a dollar. Will it stand up to the work you need it to do? What are you going to do when it breaks in the middle of a critical job? What about the computer that's slower than you need? Will you get the most out of it? Will you regret the fact you could have upgraded for a few hundred dollars more?

How Leadership Commitment Supports All Tools Available

The team identifies tools to solve a problem. Leadership must never question the need or the cost. If the team is purposeful, there won't be much additional cost. Safety or productivity will improve and far outweigh the cost of the item.

Committed leaders say: "What do you need," rather than "what does it cost?" People are encouraged to identify what's needed to do their job. Suggesting an additional location to duplicate tools goes a long way to reinforce All Tools Available.

This is not a blank checkbook. Team members know not to buy things indiscriminately. They're adults and represent the best interests of the business and those they work with. If not, they shouldn't be on the team.

Never make someone feel bad if they buy something not needed. They can always return, repurpose, donate, or dispose of it. Allow employees to err on the side of caution. They may need a tool in a fourth location, so let them buy four of the tools, rather than three.

Summary

We need tools to do our jobs, whether physically or virtually. Tools should be available where we need them, when we need them, and in the best operating condition. We rely on them. They should never let us down.

Tools must be easy to find, logically located, and simple to use. Identify the critical tools needed and make them available to anyone at any time. They must not be hidden or locked away. They need to be easily accessible.

You've notified and trained the organization in the new standard. You've provided the visuals and tools necessary to get work done in the safest and most productive manner. Now it's time to enhance alignment, buy-in, support, and commitment to the changes. Clear Benefits, the next spoke of the Wheel of Sustainability, is designed for this purpose.

All Tools Available Takeaways:

How strong Leadership Commitment supports All Tools Available:

How weak Leadership Commitment damages All Tools Available:

What I can do to improve my approach to All Tools Available:

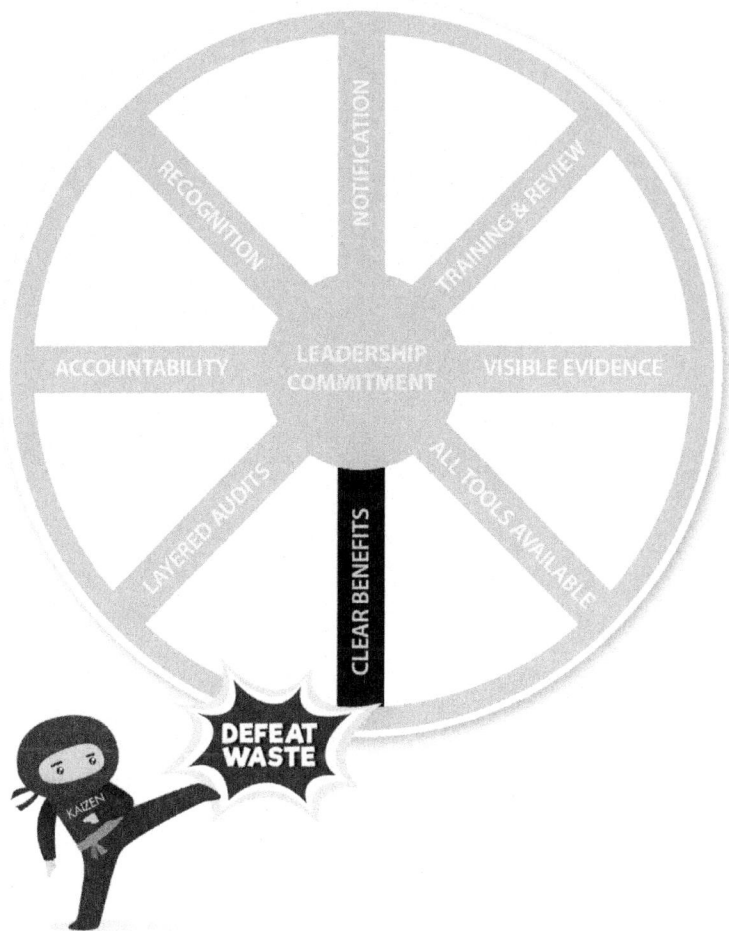

CLEAR BENEFITS

Those applying the changes must see them as simpler, safer, less stressful, and more logical in order to fully adopt them and realize the Clear Benefits.

Introduction

If someone is asked to do an unfamiliar or uncomfortable task, they'll probably reject the request out of hand. Why would they act this way? It's human nature. They expect the worst and hope for the best.

When we make changes, people naturally think negatively about changing their habits. It will be a challenge convincing them otherwise. They think their way is best. Why would they do something they didn't think was the best way to do it? They're not stupid or stubborn. If we expect them to try something new, we must convince them it's beneficial from their point of view.

Clear Benefits, the fifth spoke of the Wheel, ensures implemented changes have a direct, positive impact on the organization and the individuals working there. The team is challenged to identify the benefits of a change and then test their assumptions with others not directly involved in the improvement effort.

It's a test of the effort and resolve of the team. They'll be met with resistance. Flaws will be exposed. A strong team will welcome the knowledge and repair the flaws prior to implementation.

People will work differently if they're convinced it is a better way. Telling them about the changes won't accomplish this. Giving them the opportunity to try the changes and helping them expose and internalize the benefits is the best way.

Team members must be sold on the changes before they can sell anyone else. They must be able to visualize how safety, productivity, quality, customer service, or other key measures will improve. They must identify the Clear Benefits.

An ineffective way to change behavior is to tell people to change *"because I said so,"* or *"They're making us do it this new way."* It's not a convincing argument. It may work with small children (if even then), but not with most adults.

When we do something a certain way, we internalize the approach. We think there's a good reason we do it our way and it creates a personal benefit. Repetition reinforces behavior. Changes to our routine will feel difficult, stressful, or counterproductive.

This behavior reinforcement was used by Texaco many years ago. They told consumers to *"give us five tanks for a clean engine."* The idea was to get consumers to change their behavior by going to the local Texaco gas station five times in a row. If they did, they'd keep going there to fill up their cars. I think that was pretty clever.

You've identified the changes you want to make. You expect to be challenged. What can you do to increase your chance for a successful implementation? Communicate, communicate, and then communicate some more. Do this well before you finalize and implement the changes. Listen to the ideas, thoughts, concerns, and any other feedback you receive.

As the change is being developed, spend time reviewing the thinking with the organization. It may be challenging. People will likely reject the idea of the change without fully understanding it. It's a test of your patience and ability to communicate and demonstrate the change. It's also a test of whether or not there truly is a benefit to the person expected to follow it.

People expect the worst and hope for the best. They're focused on the negative. Flaws will be identified. Fix them prior to implementation. Promote input and feedback in the final product to reinforce Clear Benefits across the organization.

Principles of Clear Benefits

- Changes must be preferable to the person following them, from their perspective.
- The new standard is safer, simpler, less stressful, and more productive than the old way of doing things.
- Input and feedback are sought out and valued.
- Flaws are corrected prior to implementation.
- Publicize Clear Benefits to enhance buy-in and support.

Success Stories

Overcoming Resistance to Change

I was hired to help a liquid laundry detergent manufacturer cut their changeover time (the time it takes to switch materials, tooling, and equipment over from one product to another) in half. By doing so, they'd reduce inventory and overcrowding in the warehouse, shorten the time it took to service their customers, increase capacity, and raise revenues. They weren't keeping up with demand and had difficulty meeting customer orders.

Five crews operated around the clock, seven days a week. Each one believed they had the best changeover approach. The results didn't show it. There was major variation between and within crews. None were able to start up their lines consistently once the changeover was complete.

Tom, the Operations Manager, was named Team Leader. He picked a team of "All Stars" across all five crews for the $4\frac{1}{2}$ day Kaizen event. He felt their experience, creativity, and enthusiasm would lead us to a win.

This was the first changeover reduction Kaizen in the history of the plant. Team members were skeptical when we stated our objective on the first morning of the event:

Reduce the existing changeover time from 161 to 80 minutes or less, without increasing safety risk to the crew or quality risk to customers.

Team members assumed they'd have to rush, because they felt intense pressure to meet the new target time. The truth was, using *SMED* (Single Minute Exchange of Die) techniques, we'd be able to reduce enough *waste* to take significant time out and reduce safety and quality risk. Then, using the Wheel of Sustainability, we'd consistently deliver those results.

On the morning of the first day, I reviewed the four-step *SMED* methodology (with slight modifications):

Step 1 – Assess the current changeover. Identify steps done while the line is shut down (*internal steps*) and steps done while the line is still running (*external steps*).

Step 2 – Convert *internal steps* to *external steps*.

Step 3 – Streamline remaining *internal steps,* and then *external steps*.

Step 4 – Eliminate adjustments and implement the Wheel of Sustainability.

Spaghetti diagram

A technique used to identify motion required to complete a task. Using a rough drawing of an area, put your pencil down and follow the movements of someone doing work. Don't pick up the pencil until the person has completed their work. The resulting diagram has many lines and looks like spaghetti.

During Step 1, we filmed the changeover, performed motion analysis using *spaghetti diagrams*, timed and documented changeover steps, and made observations of *waste*. The team was excited by the opportunities they uncovered. They'd never stepped back to watch what was happening. They always had to participate in changeovers and focused only on what they were doing at the time. They identified many *internal* and *external* steps to convert and improve.

Next, the team identified and prioritized the steps to convert from *internal* to *external* (Step 2). They invented jigs and fixtures that allowed work to be done in preparation for the changeover, while the line was still running.

On the morning of the third day, the team tested their improvements on a simulated changeover. Time required was less than eighty minutes. They weren't satisfied. They knew they could do better.

For the rest of the day and part of the next, the team worked on improvements to streamline remaining *internal steps* (Step 3). They found ways to eliminate adjustments and created visuals to help accomplish the changeover the same way every time (Step 4). Now it was time for the ultimate test: Have another crew try the new procedure.

Each team member was assigned a crew member. They were asked to use Tell, Show, and Do (Training and Review) to review the improved method and answer any questions or concerns. They were given 1½ hours to accomplish this.

After fifteen minutes, a team member approached me.

Rose: "I really need your help. I don't know what to do."

Me: "What's going on? How can I help?"

Rose: "Vance won't review the new changeover procedure with me."

Me: "I hear he's a tough customer. Did he tell you why?"

Rose: "He's really pissed. He says we haven't listened to him and his crew."

Me: "What does Tom think about this? Can he help you?

Rose: "He's working with another pairing on the line. I don't want to bother him right now."

Me: "Okay, let me see what I can do."

We walked over to Vance. He was visibly upset. I introduced myself as the team facilitator.

Me: "What's going on Vance?"

Vance (*yelling*): *"You haven't listened to me or anyone else on the crew. You didn't film our changeover. YOU DON'T CARE WHAT WE THINK!"*

Me: "That's what we're trying to do now. Members from all crews are on the team. They're representing your interests."

Vance (*still yelling*): *"YOU'RE FEEDING ME A LOAD OF CRAP!"*

Me (*getting a little worked up*): "Look, the only way we're going to learn anything is for you to try out the new procedure and let us know what you think. Are you willing to try?"

Vance (*a little calmer*): "Really? I think you're just checking the box."

I knew I had to do something extreme or risk losing a key resource.

Me: "Are you saying you're **unwilling** to try the new procedure the team developed?"

Vance realized I had just asked him if he was being insubordinate, which is a disciplined offense in most companies.

Vance: "No, no, no. I didn't say that. I just don't like that you haven't listened to us. I'll try the new procedure and let you know what I think. I want you to know I don't think it's right and this is my protest."

Me (*with an internal sigh of relief*): "I hear you and respect your feelings. Thank you for your willingness to try the new procedure."

At 4:30 p.m., Tom gathered the crew and set the expectations for them to follow the new changeover procedure as designed. We explained they'd have the opportunity to provide feedback once the changeover was complete. Each crew member was paired with a team member, who was there to coach them, just in case they didn't remember or understand the new steps. The crew affirmed their commitment to follow the new procedure. We started the changeover at 4:40.

Three minutes later something didn't look right. One of our team members looked stressed. I motioned Julia away from her assigned crew member and asked if he wasn't following the new procedure. She nodded.

Tom and I discussed the situation. We stopped the changeover and gathered the crew to explain the issue. He told them it wasn't okay to do things the old way. We'd never learn anything about the new procedure if they did. The crew was directed to set the line back to its original condition prior to the changeover. After they did, the test would start again. Tension filled the air.

We started the second test at 5:00. In two minutes, Jack informed us his assigned crew member wasn't following the procedure. We stopped the changeover *again* and regathered the crew. Tom pleaded with them to use the new changeover procedure. He threatened to keep the test going, even if it took all night. Was this day ever going to end?

After resetting the line, we started the third changeover attempt. This time, everyone followed the new procedure. Tension faded away and was replaced by exhaustion. Team members had been working since 6:30.

Sixty-five minutes later, the changeover was complete and the line was running smoothly. We brought everyone into a meeting room to review the crew's feedback and reaction to the new procedure. I was curious to see how Vance and his mates would respond to the changes and the two stoppages we imposed when they went *rogue*.

We gathered around a flip chart. Each crew member was asked to highlight what they liked and issues to be improved. As they spoke, I wrote their comments for everyone to see.

Vance started out the feedback session by telling us he *"loved"* four improvements made by the team:

1. He easily found what he needed.
2. He didn't have to carry tools with him.
3. He didn't feel rushed.
4. He felt the new procedure was safer and more logical.

He then offered constructive feedback on things we could improve. Others shared similar feedback. Everyone had positive and constructive things to say.

I admit I was a little surprised by the positive tone in the room. I figured the crew would save up all of their anger for the feedback session. Instead, they were appreciative for the team's efforts. They realized the team was representing their interests. The test proved it to them. They identified Clear Benefits of the changes.

We thanked everyone, and sent them back to the line or home. There were handshakes, fist bumps, and high fives on their way out. I was exhausted and exhilarated by the roller coaster ride of the day. I was thankful to go home and get some rest.

At the report out to leadership, the team explained the importance of gathering input and testing out new ideas with a group not involved in the improvement effort. They highlighted how difficult change can be. They stayed true to their convictions and implemented something with Clear Benefits to the organization. Since then, the line has sustained the reduced changeover time and created additional believers in changeover reduction and Kaizen.

Reliability Kaizen

Designed to improve the performance of a manufacturing operation using centering, leveling, balancing, squaring, and physics principles. Teams learn simple ways to make mechanical improvements and then use the Wheel of Sustainability to sustain the improved performance.

There Is One Best Way

A laundry detergent manufacturer in Missouri hired me to run a Reliability Kaizen event. In preparation, I conducted a site visit and took a Gemba walk of the line to be improved. Cluttered, dirty, and lacking organization, the line was operating at low efficiency levels. An hourly production board was filled with red numbers, indicating output was consistently below target levels. Working with the sponsor, we aligned around the approach to improve safety and productivity.

After chartering the $4\frac{1}{2}$ day event, I coached the team leader, Jeff (Operations Manager), around assembling the ideal team:

- Production operators from all four crews.
- Two maintenance mechanics.
- Anyone else wanting to make the line better and learn reliability improvement methods.
- Team members from other locations who had demonstrated their passion and willingness to help teams win (*Kaizen Rock Stars*).

Two weeks before the event, we had commitment from all team members, including two *Kaizen Rock Stars*, who were traveling to the plant from hundreds of miles away. Two production supervisors and one engineer also joined the team.

On the morning of the first day, team members introduced themselves and reviewed their prior improvement experience. Kaizen was new for half of the team. They weren't sure what to expect and were skeptical we'd be able to make meaningful improvements.

After a Lean and Reliability overview, we Gemba walked to the line to observe performance and generate safety and other improvement ideas. The team was directed to focus on equipment reliability, using principles and techniques we had just reviewed.

We returned to the meeting room with more than one hundred ideas. That's an encouraging number generated by a team with little Kaizen experience. A majority of the ideas focused on two areas of the line: carton wrapping and container filling.

The team prioritized carton wrapping as the highest source of stress, safety risk, and downtime, so we decided to work on it first. We shut the line down and locked it out. Then, we started working on our reliability improvements.

Knowing we would be working on the container filler next, we asked the crew on shift to deep clean it during the shutdown. There was so much dirt, grime, and excess laundry detergent powder, it was difficult to see the equipment underneath.

The conveyer leading to the carton wrapper had three lanes available for products to travel in. There were two lanes of containers being wrapped.

Me: "I'm curious. I see two containers going down the conveyers. But there are three lanes. When do you use the third lane?"

Jane (operator): "Now that you ask, I've been here many years and I've never seen it used."

Robert (mechanic): "I installed this line. We've never used the third lane."

Me: "Okay, let's think about this. The equipment is designed to wrap two filled containers. Is that right?"

Robert: "Sure is. We couldn't wrap three if we wanted to."

Me: "So, let me get this straight. There's a third lane and you never use it. Is it in your way?"

Jane: "Always. Every time I have to fix a problem or clear a jam, I have to reach over the third lane. It's a real pain."

Me: "If we know we never have and never will use it, can we remove the third lane?"

Team: "*HELL YES!*"

And just like that, the lane was gone. The line was less cluttered, safer to run, and simpler to maintain.

Next, we found the center of the carton wrapper and measured the two lanes inside of it. They were 1" off-center. Although that doesn't sound like much, it was enough to contribute to jams and line stops. We rebalanced them. Then, we relocated the lanes leading into the carton wrapper to match.

We restarted the line and sent test containers through the newly balanced equipment. They flowed more smoothly than anyone on the team had ever experienced. They were becoming believers in reliability improvement methods.

There were many more improvements to be made on the carton wrapper, but I knew we could get more work completed if we split up our resources. Half of the team turned their attention to the container filler.

Newly cleaned, we were able to see some of the parts in the filler weren't correct. Parts used for the large-size container were mixed in with small-size container parts. Most were in a state of disrepair. These critical problems had been hidden by dust, dirt, and spilled laundry detergent powder.

We knew what we had to do: Put the proper parts in the filler, repair any broken ones, and create a visual system to keep the wrong parts out of the filler. Mechanics spent hours repairing broken container filler parts. While that work was in process, we made improvements to other portions of the line.

After all major improvements were completed, it was time to determine the best way to set up and run the line. We had to standardize across all crews. This is a critical and challenging step. Most operators think their way is the best way.

I took Jeff aside and reviewed the strategy for standardization. We'd meet with all of the operators and facilitate them to an agreement on a new procedure. With so many changes and improvements to the line, the old methods were no longer relevant.

The four operators didn't see it that way. Two in particular, Sue and Jane, thought their way was best. The other two didn't agree, but weren't willing to argue as passionately or loudly. After thirty minutes of discussing and arguing, Sue and Jane believed their different methods produced the same results. I knew this wasn't the case.

We had to commit to a new standard procedure. I asked Sue and Jane to demonstrate their methods separately. Jeff and the two operators would observe and measure both using *spaghetti diagrams* and timing. The *spaghetti diagram* measures the distance a person travels when they're doing their work. Timing measures the duration of the effort. Analysis, rather than emotion, would tell us the best way to proceed.

Sue and Jane were instructed to work at a comfortable pace, without putting themselves at risk. It was more important to learn the best way and do it in a way that would make it easy to train others. The observers were responsible to identify further improvements. Sue confidently went first.

She worked clockwise around the line, performing all required tasks. A few times she overlooked the changes. We stopped the clock to remind her of what she missed. We restarted the clock after she corrected her errors. Sue finished in twenty-five minutes. She was sure her way was best.

Jane was next. She worked counterclockwise around the line. She followed the new steps in an efficient and stress-free manner. She didn't have to walk far to accomplish any steps and didn't forget anything. It looked simple and natural. Fourteen minutes later she was finished.

The team was shocked. They didn't think there'd be so much difference. Sue spoke of the Clear Benefits of Jane's approach. This was a breakthrough. All four operators agreed to support and represent the new method to their co-workers. I reinforced the notion that strong commitment to the changes would keep the line running well from now on.

At the report out, Sue and Jane admitted they had to be open to thinking differently and there was always a better way to get things done. The team was proud of their accomplishments and the plant had a safer and more reliable process. One month later, I received a text from Jeff. He shared a photo of the hourly production board, filled with green numbers.

Breaking Through the Edge

Sometimes a change is so impactful and deeply moving, the organization sees the Clear Benefits from the beginning. This is one of those stories.

Many years ago, I was assigned to help a team reduce the changeover time of a painting operation at a ceiling tile plant in Oregon. The goal was to reduce the existing changeover time by 50 percent or more, while improving safety.

After reviewing Lean principles and *SMED* techniques, we took a Gemba walk to observe a changeover in progress and generate improvement ideas. The team identified dozens of improvement opportunities. They were excited to help everyone in the process to achieve their goals.

Towards the end of the Gemba walk, we stopped at the quality testing station and saw something that didn't look right to us. Marie, the Quality Technician, was cutting four two-foot edges of a ceiling tile off with a box knife. It was difficult, unsafe, and inefficient. When asked about it, she told us she was required to measure the color of the painted face and edges to verify they matched.

The only way to measure the color was to make the cuts, allowing the tester to be placed directly on the edges. Marie told us it made her wrists hurt at the end of the day. I was told plant leadership was very concerned about this difficult task. It was their current top safety concern. Engineers had studied the issue but hadn't yet identified a practical solution.

We returned to the meeting room and listed all of our improvement ideas. We prioritized the ideas with the highest impact on changeover time. During the next two days, the highest priority ideas were implemented. We were excited about our progress.

At a break on the third day, Dave, a mechanic on the team, approached me.

Dave: "Is it okay to work on something that won't reduce changeover time?"

Me: "That depends on what you want to do. What's going on?"
Dave: "I can't get the edge cutting process out of my mind. It's not right. We're putting people at risk. It needs to be fixed. It's our top safety problem."

Me: "Safety improvement is one of our objectives. Do you have an idea of how to solve the problem?"

Dave: "I think so. If you give me some time to work on my idea, I'll come back and help with other projects."

Me: "I think that's reasonable. Let's see what everyone else thinks."

Kaizen is a team sport. There needs to be alignment around what everyone is doing. Team members enthusiastically supported Dave's efforts. Fred, an operator on the team, volunteered to help Dave. We were anxious to see what they'd come up with.

An hour and half later, Dave and Fred came back with grins a mile wide. They brought a vise with a two-foot-wide angle iron attached to each jaw. We stopped our work to watch a demonstration of their invention. They placed a ceiling tile into the vise vertically, with the edge of the tile in the jaws and closed it carefully. With a swift tap, the ceiling tile broke off cleanly at the edge, across the entire two-foot length.

We were stunned. One of our team members stepped up and tried the next ceiling tile edge. It broke off just as cleanly. One by one, we all tried it and saw how quick and easy it was to use. Then, we gave it the ultimate test. We brought it to Marie and showed her how to use it. She easily broke off the edge and gave Dave a hug in a show of gratitude. It was likely the first hug he got at the plant.

We were proud of Dave's invention. There was much work yet to do. We had to finish our other changeover reduction projects and build standard work for the new procedure. We also had to gain alignment from plant leadership that our new edge breaking method would meet strict quality testing requirements.

During the remainder of our time, we implemented as many improvements as possible. Then, we created an overall changeover procedure which we verified, practiced, and used to train the rest of the crew. Changeover time was cut in half. We knew it wouldn't be a total victory unless we installed the new edge breaking process. We built our final report to win over the leadership team.

We invited plant leadership to see the new changeover procedure, which the team demonstrated. Some of the leadership team participated, to see for themselves how much easier and safer it had become. They were pleased. Little did they know, we saved the best demonstration for last.

Dave invited Marie to join him in front of the audience. Then, Fred brought out the vise and handed a ceiling tile to her. She put it in the vise, gave it a tap, and the edge broke right off, as clean as could be. In my life, I'd never seen a collective group of people's jaws drop at the same time as happened right then. After they got over their initial shock, our Sponsor said, "Let me try that." He did, and got the same result.

Everyone wanted a turn. When they were finished, the HR Manager said, "This has been our number one safety risk. We've spent months trying to solve it the conventional way and haven't been able to. Your team worked together and solved it this week. We need more teams to help us solve our problems in this way. Thank you!" She gave Dave a hug.

Blushing, Dave admitted that in all of his years working at the plant, he had never done anything as impactful. He also reminded us this was a "*prototype*" and there might be a better way to break the edges off. Many years later, the original *prototype* was still being used without a complaint.

Less than Success Story

A Wake-Up Call

I was the Business Unit Manager at a Vinyl Flooring Plant in Pennsylvania for two years. Responsible for one of four business units on site, I led a unionized workforce of 160 employees, three supervisors, and eight technical staff. My job was to turn the shrinking business around and keep my employees safe and productive.

With many layoffs over the years, the least tenured hourly employees had more than twenty-five years of service. They had seen many Business Unit Managers come and go. All three supervisors had been promoted from the ranks, and were of the mindset to survive until the next Business Unit Manager arrived.

> **Lock out Tag out**
>
> *An OSHA mandated program used to keep employees from risking severe injury or death when interacting with equipment that has stored energy. Employees are trained and held accountable to eliminate any sources of stored energy and keep them secured while servicing equipment.*

This wasn't the ideal situation to drive change, but we had to do many things better, and fast. One such change was to do a better job protecting our employees. We instituted a stronger safety program with improvements in the way employees interacted with and *locked-out* their equipment. We were convinced we were doing the right thing, but we had major pushback from the union and the supervisors, who believed the new requirements were a waste of time and effort. After much discussion, my staff and supervisors agreed to be consistent in our safety message, approach, and accountability. At least that's what I thought.

One morning, I overheard one of the supervisors telling his crew they needed to follow the new safety protocols because, "*The company is making me do this.*" Much to my concern and disappointment, his statement confirmed he didn't see the Clear Benefits of the changes. I knew he would never hold himself or his crew accountable to follow the enhanced safety requirements.

I couldn't let this continue and immediately stepped in. I corrected the situation and sent him packing. It sounds harsh. There's much more to this story. He had been demonstrating a pattern of subversive and destructive behavior for months. This was the final straw. I was unwilling to put employees at risk and knew a change had to be made.

Although firing someone can be a life changing event for them and those they work with, it ended up turning out fairly well for everyone involved. The remaining supervisors and crew took safety more seriously. The terminated supervisor later admitted this was a wake-up call for him.

Clear Benefits at Home or in the Office

People do things at home that make sense to them. Sometimes conditions change and the way we do things needs to change as well. It happened to me when I opened my consulting firm, Process Improvement Partners LLC.

I wouldn't be working from my prior employer's office. Home was my new workplace. Where was I going to work? Every room in the house had a purpose and was furnished appropriately.

My wife and I chose the living room. This was the least used room in the house. There was furniture in the room that wasn't conducive to a home-based business. We relocated or donated it. The next step was to determine what I needed to help me do my job in the most efficient way.

I needed a desk, laptop, printer, and other supplies. After doing research, I bought what I thought would help me do my work. I decided to display critical business information (Visible Evidence). Using existing wall space and determining the type of information to be displayed, I ordered a three by four-foot white board.

Once it arrived, I experimented with various information display designs. Eventually, I settled on a system that would be simple and helpful to me first, and to my wife next.

I mounted the board at an ergonomic height (top edge at 68" and bottom edge at 34"). Next, I designed a two-week calendar, broken up by days of the week. It helps me keep my current schedule in front of me and gives my wife a way to know where I am supposed to be at all times. I put that information across the board, from Sunday to Saturday, at the top of the board. Below the calendar, I designed sections focused on current critical tasks, business acquisition measures, and content development progress.

Over the years, I've refined the information in each of those sections to be more helpful and quicker to read. I know the value of seeing this information every day. It keeps me focused on the things that help me build and maintain my business. My wife stops by to look at the board frequently. She asks me relevant and critical questions based on displayed information. This forces me to keep things current and reinforces the value of the board. I do not doubt the Clear Benefits of having this valuable tool to run my business.

How to Develop Effective Clear Benefits

Changes should positively impact safety, quality, productivity, customer experience, profitability, or other critical business or performance measures. A positive safety result shouldn't negatively affect another factor, such as productivity. This is the challenge for a team to come up with creative ways to accomplish. Once they meet the challenge, they need to consider all of the following aspects to identify and communicate the Clear Benefits.

Reasons for the changes

- What was the problem the team was trying to solve and why was it perceived to be a problem?
- What would the customer say about the problem?
- What would the organization say about the problem?
- What would the person directly impacted by the problem in their normal work say?
- What might inform us the change is for the better?
- Why does the change matter to the customer, employees, organization, shareholders?

Benefits of the changes

Put yourself in the shoes of the person who may feel they had no input to the change. What will be perceived as a benefit? What's in it for them? Teams get married to the changes they're making. They know why they did what they did. They've seen the benefits of it by performing experiments and trials. They're convinced. Now you need to identify benefits that will be easy to see and feel from the perspective of someone who has no knowledge of or input to the changes.

Test changes early and often

Test the changes well before they're finalized. When you have an idea of what you want to do, experiment. Don't wait for things to be perfect or final. The more you test the changes, the more you'll expose more issues and create opportunities to improve. Try something when it is 60 percent complete. Don't wait for 100 percent.

Gather extensive feedback

Ask as many people as possible to provide input to the changes. Even if you're just describing what you're considering, many will be happy to tell you what they think. Don't be shocked by negative feedback. Use it to make improvements. Those outside of the team will appreciate being heard and may support the implementation of the changes in ways you don't expect.

How will the benefits manifest themselves?

Will we be able to touch, see, or feel the benefits? Is there a way to make them obvious? Are there visuals, metrics, or other indicators to help others see the benefits and internalize them? If people tell others, you have a better chance to sustain the changes. Recognition (spoke 8) reinforces the value of the change shared through stories.

Measure the change

What does the evidence say about the change? Are there objective and/or subjective measures? Can those measures be displayed so everyone will see them (Visible Evidence)? Is there anecdotal evidence? Those creating the changes must determine ways to visualize, measure, and validate the changes are for the better.

Demonstrate cause and effect

Once a change is made, demonstrate its direct impact on positive results. Make it easy to connect the changes to improvements in safety, productivity, customer service, or any other critical performance measure. Visualize the "before" and "after" conditions. Take photos and post them prominently.

Commit to the change

How long are you willing to follow the change without making modifications? What's the length of the "*let's see how it goes*" time? Do you have leadership and organizational alignment to stick with the changes as developed? What will you do if unintended safety or productivity issues arise?

Mistakes to Avoid

Not asking for input or feedback

The team is married to their ideas. They haven't asked anyone outside of the team what they think. They assume everyone else knows and understands their thinking. People think the worst and hope for the best. Because of this, they will naturally view any changes as negative. If you don't give people a chance to provide input or feedback, they'll have no reason to adjust their thinking.

Testing changes on people who won't challenge thinking

You won't learn much if the people you test changes on aren't willing to tell you what they really think. We don't want "yes-men" and "yes-women". We want to expose issues.

Not testing the changes in a real-world setting

Everything looks good on paper or in a meeting room. How will it work in a real situation? If the team doesn't test the changes in context, they will miss vital issues, problems, or learning. Others will have no idea what to expect. The real world is three-dimensional. There are infinite variables. People are the biggest variable. Test the changes in the actual process.

Waiting until it's too late to make improvements

The team wants everything to be perfect prior to rolling out changes. People aren't perfect. If you wait to test the changes, you'll miss vital learning and opportunity to make improvements based on the results. Test early and often.

Ignoring the connection between the changes and results

Even if the changes cause something positive to happen, if you ignore them or don't make them visible, others won't relate the changes to a positive outcome. Don't waste this opportunity.

Not measuring the impact of the changes

If you don't test the changes and measure their impact, there's no way of knowing if they will improve the current conditions or make them worse.

How Leadership Commitment Supports Clear Benefits

Leaders will be approached by employees when changes are made. Not everyone will understand the reasons for the changes. People are familiar and comfortable with the current way they do things. Why would they want to adjust their behavior?

Leaders must be firm in their convictions that the changes are in the best interests of the employees, their customers, and the organization. They must be able to explain and describe the benefits. What is the cause and effect? How have things improved? Why are we better off? Why is it not okay to deviate from the new standard?

Strong leaders demonstrate commitment by being familiar enough with the changes that they can personally demonstrate the benefits. They don't delegate these discussions to others. They look people in the eye and share their reasons for supporting the changes. The more they personalize the benefits, the more their commitment strengthens.

Look for evidence of the positive impact of the changes and share it with anyone who will listen. Tell stories of the changes and how they improved results for the organization (Recognition). Initiate conversations. Find people who are opposed to the new standard and listen to their feedback and input. Take the time to explain why you believe the changes are helpful and necessary. Give the gift of your time, especially when improvements are fresh. Dissatisfied customers will eventually find you. Find them first and help them navigate the changes.

Summary

We develop improvements to make things simpler, safer, and less stressful for the organization and its customers. Not everyone sees it that way. Clear Benefits drives you to identify the impact of the new standard work from the perspective of those who will be required to follow it. If they're not on board, the improvements won't stick. Gather input, feedback, and test the changes from the perspective of your internal customers.

If things go well, most people will see and feel the benefits of the changes immediately. Others won't buy in right away. Be strong in your convictions of the benefits, so that you can make them clear and obvious to others. If you do, the organization will follow your lead and commit to the new standard.

Even though you've identified the Clear Benefits of the changes and everyone is on board, you can't relax. People may still return to their old habits and ways of doing things. That's where the next spoke comes in. Layered Audits will help identify when people are doing things the way they should or if they're deviating from the standard.

Clear Benefits Takeaways:

How strong Leadership Commitment supports Clear Benefits:

How weak Leadership Commitment damages Clear Benefits:

What I can do to improve my approach to Clear Benefits:

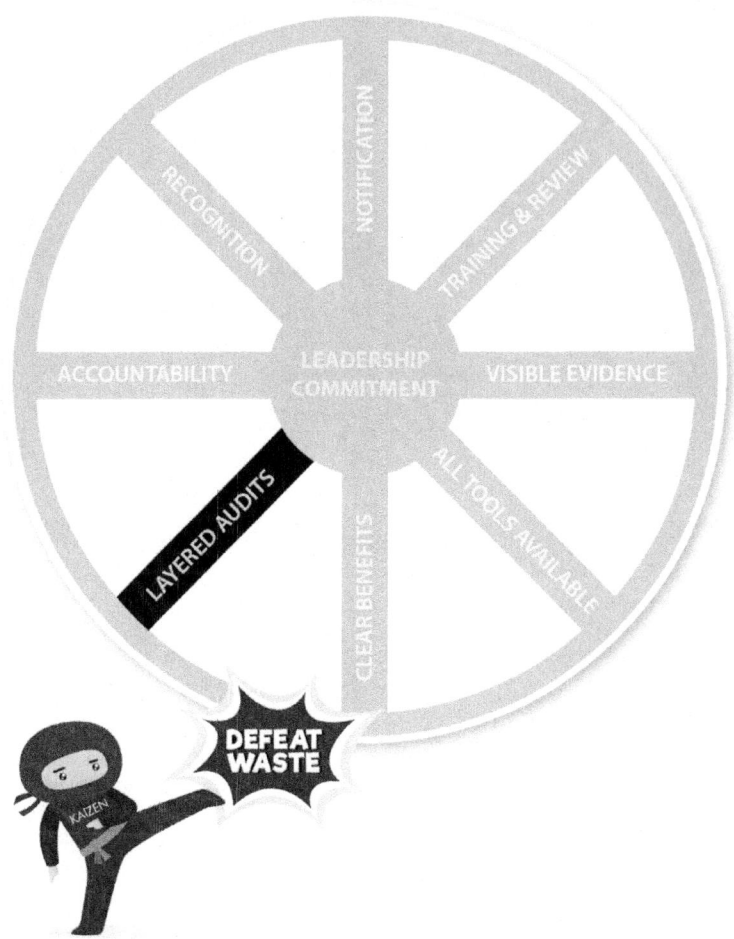

LAYERED AUDITS

5S Audit Sheet

Area: _____   Auditor: _____   Date: _____

	Item Description	5S Evaluation and Scoring Criteria	Score (0-5)	Notes for next level of improvement — Any score of 4 or less requires comment
		0 = 5+ problems 2 = 3 problems 4 = 1 problems 1 = 4 problems 3 = 2 problems 5 = 0 problems		
SORT	No unnecessary items	All items not necessary for performing work are removed from the workplace (i.e., parts, WIP, tools, equipment, furniture) ; only needed tools and products are present at work stations. No items are on top of machines, cabinets, or equipment. Tripping dangers are removed from walking area.		
	Documentation and binders	Only binders containing documentation necessary for operations (such as MSDS and SOP binders) are stored at the workstation. Only required paperwork present and outdated posters, announcements etc. are removed.		
SET IN ORDER	Material storage	Boxes, containers and materials are necessary and stored neatly in clearly labeled shelves or cabinets. WIP and other small items are not stored on the floor. Large items are stored on the floor in color-coded designated area. Stacked items are not crooked or leaning over.		
	Equipment, tools and gages	Equipment & furniture is clearly identified & in designated location. Tools, fixtures & gages are stored neatly in designated locations at ergo friendly height, within reach of operator; storage is designed to ensure cleanliness & prevent		
	Cleaning equipment & mtrl.	All cleaning equipment and material are easily accessible and stored neatly in clearly labeled locations (color coded, easily visible, and easily accessible)		
	Emergency equipment	Fire fighting and other emergency/first aid equipment is unobstructed and correctly stored in color coded area. Emergency stop switches/breakers are		

Layered Audits are used to engage with those doing the work to ensure it is done properly and is well understood. Auditors immediately provide help and support when faced with deviations from standard.

Introduction

There's a negative association with the word *audit*. Put it next to IRS and the first thought is: **RUN**!

I visited a pharmaceutical company in Montreal. During a Gemba walk, I asked questions of those I met along the way. I think I'm personable and easy to talk to. Everyone kept their answers short and acted as if everything was fine. When my tour guide explained I wasn't an auditor, people opened up and told me what they really thought. Things weren't fine.

No wonder people avoid audits. What they may not realize is: audits can be designed to be helpful, easy to accomplish, and encourage two-way learning.

In this chapter, I'll help you develop Layered Audits that support the organization, are easy to conduct, create learning opportunities, and sustain critical changes.

After I completed my Industrial Engineering degree at Virginia Tech, I started my career at a furniture company in North Carolina. My first assignment was to study workflow in a veneer factory. The purpose was to rebalance tasks and improve efficiency. I carried a clipboard and documented my observations.

I walked through the plant at random times, identified who was working, who wasn't, and took notes. Employees looked at me with concern and skepticism. Some thought I was a spy. Others asked if I was going to buy the company. I was a young engineer. How was I going to buy a company?

People didn't trust me. They yelled, whistled, and called me names. That is, until I explained what I was doing. It defused the situation and created more positive engagements. Employees opened up, treated me as an equal, showed me what was going on, and shared improvement ideas. That experience taught me to create a more engaging and inclusive approach to auditing.

The first step was to identify the reasons to conduct a system audit:

- Determine if the system is operating properly, not putting people at risk, and well understood.
- Reinforce its importance.
- Uncover issues and identify improvement opportunities.
- Correct counterproductive behaviors and provide help.

Once the reasons are understood, design the audit using these rules of thumb:

- The audit takes no more than five minutes to conduct.
- It's interactive, helpful, and promotes two-way learning.
- It's inclusive of anyone working in the system.
- It includes a sign-off.
- Create layers of audit responsibility.

No more than five minutes to conduct – Five minutes is a challenging, but achievable, target. It's hard to object to something that adds so little time, especially if it adds value. Total time includes review of the system and engagement with those doing the work. Only review critical system elements during the audit. Don't try to audit everything. Stay focused. If you can't cover everything in a single audit, rotate areas and elements in subsequent audits.

Interactive, helpful, and promotes two-way learning – Explain what you're doing, ask questions, and share findings with those you encounter during the audit. Don't observe from afar. If the audit looks like help, people will welcome you and share ideas to improve the system. You may learn something you can apply elsewhere.

Inclusive of anyone working in the system – Avoid auditing only *when* it's convenient for you, such as 8:30 every morning, or *where* it's convenient for you, such as outside your office. Be flexible and audit at random times, areas, or processes. Rotate through people, so that it doesn't feel like you're focusing on a specific person or group. Don't include everyone in the audit, unless it can be done without rushing. Don't personally conduct every audit. Use Training and Review (spoke 2) to help others conduct the audit on your behalf.

Sign-off – People need to know you took the time to audit their system. If they don't see or engage with you, they may never know you were there. You want to reinforce the importance of the system to everyone. Sign off and indicate you were there and you care enough to help and support them. Sign-offs create Visible Evidence (spoke 3) and auditor Accountability (spoke 7).

Create layers – Different levels of the organization support the system in different ways through layers of responsibility and audit frequency.

Layer One

The person doing the work audits their work as they do it. They uncover problems and resolve them immediately. They have the most critical eye and know all details.

Frequency: Continuously and hourly.

Layer Two

The supervisor or manager of the person doing the work audits on a less frequent basis. They are responsible for overall compliance to the standard. They have responsibility for the daily performance and safety of their team. They should also have enough knowledge and experience to help if there are any issues or problems uncovered during the audit.

Frequency: Daily.

Layer Three

The manager of all supervisors/managers assesses the quality of the audit conducted by those reporting to them. They randomly check elements in the system being audited to verify findings and compliance to the standard.

Frequency: Weekly.

Beyond Layer Three

Layers continue until the organization runs out of levels of responsibility. Executives should audit on a quarterly or yearly basis.

All levels are engaged to drive and support the most critical systems and changes. Keep audits fresh by rotating times, people, aspects of the system, areas of the organization, and auditors.

Developing effective audits doesn't have to be difficult. Many people think of audits as additional paperwork, waste, or a pain in the neck. The rest of this chapter will help you overcome resistance to Layered Audits.

Principles of Layered Audits

- Use Layered Audits to assess the health of a system.
- Deviations from standard are immediately corrected through support and help.
- Commitment is demonstrated through audit interactions and engagement.
- Audits promote two-way learning.
- Everyone can be an auditor. All levels in the organization participate.

Success Stories

Owning Their Solution in the Weld Shop

I have conducted dozens of 5S Kaizen events. The results are always dramatic. All teams consisted of production operators or office workers, and included one or two mechanics. Production operators or office workers owned the areas to be improved. The mechanics completed more complex tasks.

That changed when I met my Weld shop team. The team was comprised of five mechanics and an engineer. Something amazing was about to happen.

Let me tell you about a typical mechanic on a Kaizen team. They think they're there to support the team. They don't always feel invested in the improvement process or the area being worked on. Most of the time, they participate in the Kaizen and do great work. Sometimes they aren't interested in being there, and would rather be doing their "*normal*" job.

Facilitating a team with some members who felt this way wasn't new for me. An entire team with this mindset was. The good news was the area to be worked on directly impacted the safety and productivity of all team members. The better news was that Craig was the team leader. He was the mechanical supervisor and was passionate about improving conditions in the Weld shop. The best news was team pride and competitive nature could be leveraged to turn the Weld shop into a showplace. But only if they were willing to own and sustain the improvements.

When I facilitate a 5S Kaizen, I work one S at a time. On the first day of the Kaizen, after training the team, we took a Gemba walk into the Weld shop. I directed the team to identify things we could remove – the clutter. This is the first S, Sort. We must have removed more than 80 percent of items in the shop. We filled a large scrap metal dumpster.

Next, we determined optimal locations for anything remaining. Using a shared work table as the focal point, team members demonstrated how each new location improved their safety and productivity. This is Set in Order, the second S.

We made sure everything was in the best possible condition. We cleaned and inspected all tools, equipment, materials, surfaces, and storage spaces. If something was in disrepair, we fixed or replaced it. Everything had to work at peak performance. This is Shine, the third S.

The first three S's – Sort, Set in Order, and Shine – are the most physical, dramatic, and fun parts of the Kaizen event. The space was dramatically different from the morning of the first day.

Here's an example: Prior to the event, employees entered the Weld shop and walked thirty feet in the dark to turn on the lights. They navigated through clutter in the hope of finding the switch without banging into or tripping over something.

In the *before* photos, the light switch was hidden behind large metal sheets leaning against the wall. At the end of the second day, we relocated the switch to the entrance of the Weld shop. Lights could now be turned on before entering the shop, eliminating a critical safety risk. The team went home on a high note. I planned to introduce Standardize and Sustain, the fourth and fifth S, the next morning.

The team had everything in the shop as they wanted it. The challenge was to create a managing system to keep it that way. Requirements had to be established and followed by everyone using the Weld shop in the future.

This was not a physical exercise. It was to be accomplished through the use of visualization, and Layered Audits. To mechanics, this is *paperwork*. It might as well be a four-letter word.

This was the last thing the team wanted to work on, and I knew it. But it was a critical step. Improvements would deteriorate if we didn't take Standardize and Sustain seriously. The key was for the team to own their solution and not just go through the motions. I had a plan and it was risky: if necessary, facilitate an emotional event to drive the team to create and own their managing system.

When the team arrived on the third day, I congratulated them for their achievements. Next, I explained it was *"Standardize and Sustain Day"*. Grumpy faces met my review of checklists and audits developed by other Kaizen teams.

They weren't impressed. They didn't believe *paperwork* would keep people from destroying their good work. I explained teams made these documents visible and established responsibility and alignment all the way up to leadership. They were still not buying it. I needed to push them further.

I displayed a PowerPoint slide of an example audit. As I reviewed requirements line by line, there was discomfort and frustration on their faces. On line six of the audit, Sammy, the lead welder and Area Owner, stood up. His face was beet red.

"Adam, we've had enough of your *paperwork*. We're going to the Smoke Shack and you're not invited. *We'll* figure it out and then *we'll* tell you what we're going to do."

They stormed off. I had facilitated an emotional event. Although this was my plan, I wasn't sure they'd come back. If they did, what would they decide to do? I hoped they'd return soon.

It felt like hours, but it was only twenty minutes later when they returned. They looked proud of themselves. Craig declared, "Adam, we've come to a decision. *We'll talk, you type.*"

They listed eleven requirements for *their* audit. Although it was similar to what I'd presented earlier, it was in their words. That's all that mattered. I thanked them for coming up with a strong audit and then challenged them to develop the system to ensure it would be used properly and not *"pencil-whipped"*.

Now enthusiastic and focused on the win, the team developed an Area Owner board, with required documents that were easy to find and use. They included a photo of Sammy to drive their ownership and accountability message. They developed a three-Layered Audit, with requirements for the area users, Sammy, and members of the leadership team.

At the report out, results were shared with the plant leadership team and visiting executives. Mechanics typically resist presenting in front of an audience. In this case, they didn't and everyone spoke from their hearts and explained how important it was to support and sustain their good work. It improved safety and productivity for them and the rest of the employees in the plant. They asked the executives to hold leadership accountable to keep this good thing going and expand the effort to other areas of the plant.

After the presentation, I spent time with the team, listening to their feedback on their week. Happy with the results and most aspects of the Kaizen, they told me they wished I had been more assertive. They laughed as I told them I wasn't sure they were coming back after storming out of the meeting room. They told me it was the motivation they needed to reach their solution.

Gemba Walks

For those unfamiliar with the term, Gemba means *"the real place, the place where the work is done."* A Gemba walk means to walk through the real place and assess the work being done there. My interpretation is: walk through and assess the health of the operating system. If this sounds

like an audit, that's because it is. Think of it as a Layer Three audit.

The idea is to take leaders out of their offices and walk through the process with their employees. It's not always the most comfortable thing to do. If done well, it can be extremely impactful. If not done well, it's a waste of time. The idea is to make a Gemba walk as engaging and value-adding as possible. The next story describes how a team developed a Gemba walk that drove organizational behavior and performance to levels they were hoping for.

I was the Production Manager at an Oregon ceiling tile plant for three years. I tested and applied continuous improvement principles directly to a manufacturing organization and received immediate feedback. I applied my approach in a way that supported and enhanced the strong team culture at the plant.

I spent a significant portion of my time walking the manufacturing floor, engaging with the technicians and mechanics, and auditing the systems that kept us safe and productive. We used many paper documents. Technicians were required to sign off when they completed critical tasks. Team Managers audited their crews on a daily basis. I reviewed their audits weekly. We were 100 percent compliant for critical task completion for a year and a half. The plant was operating at peak efficiency and set the all-time company performance record in the middle of my tenure (see the related story in Chapter 2 – *Attention to Detail*).

Due to an economic downturn, staffing was reduced. I was offered a position at the corporate office in Pennsylvania. I hated to leave the West Coast, but knew it was the right decision for my family. I felt the plant would continue operating well, using the systems developed during my time there. Sadly, this was not the case.

Productivity started to suffer. The plant recognized this and implemented a daily staff-led Gemba walk. After many months, performance didn't improve. I was invited to visit the plant to help. I was happy to return. I missed my team on the West Coast.

I attended the Gemba walk and observed interactions and engagements with the technicians. Eleven staff members walked through the factory, stopping at designated locations to engage with the technician performing a task. At each stop, they asked two questions:

1.   Is everything okay?
2.   Do you need any help from us?

Most of the time, the technician would say everything was okay (it wasn't) and they didn't need help (they did). The person asking the questions engaged with the technician. The rest of the group didn't seem to know their role. They didn't pay much attention to what was going on. After the questions were answered, they'd thank the technician and walk to another location.

Roger, the Manufacturing Manager, asked my opinion of what I observed.

Roger: "You know us pretty well. What do you think about our Gemba walk?"

Me: "Before I answer that, I need to know: What is the purpose of your Gemba walk?"

Roger: "Support and help our technicians stay safe, productive, and identify issues that are in their way."

Me: "If that's your purpose, your Gemba walk isn't helping you accomplish it."

Roger: "I'm not sure I understand. What do you mean?"

Me: "The technicians don't believe you're there to support and help them. Their short answers to your questions tell me that."

Roger: "Is anything else bothering you about our Gemba walk?"

Me: "The staff isn't engaging. It's troubling and disrespectful to the technicians."

Roger: "Wow, that's a pretty tough critique. What do you suggest we do about it?"

Me: "Let's create a Gemba walk that achieves your purpose."

Roger: "I'm in. What do you need me to do?"

Me: "Assemble a team to help us. We need technicians, Team Managers, and some staff. If you can pull them together, we can start tomorrow morning."

Roger: "It's short notice, but I can get it done. We'll be ready."

The next morning, we reviewed Gemba walk principles:

- Help those you engage and interact with.
- Assess the health of the operating system.
- Engage and support the technicians. They're your internal customers.

Next, the team was challenged to develop expectations for their Gemba walk. They identified three:

1. Prioritize and take action on the top issues impacting safety and productivity.
2. Expose issues the technicians are overlooking in their everyday work.
3. Support, engage, and provide help to the technicians.

The first step in designing the new Gemba walk was to improve the questions to increase engagement and exposure of issues. They weren't yes or no questions anymore. Now, they were "*show me*" questions. These are some examples:

- "Show me the problem that shut down the line yesterday."
- "Show me the safety issue that concerns you the most."
- "Show me how the valve works when you switch paint from tank A to tank B."

In order to expose risks and increase engagement, we identified specific roles for Gemba walk team members:

1. Note taker
2. Standard work reviewer
3. 5S observer

4. Operations viewer
5. Scrap moderator
6. Maintenance technician
7. Production technician

Responsibilities were written on seven cards to be handed out randomly at the beginning of the Gemba walk. At designated stops, findings were to be reviewed with the technicians. At the end of the walk, the team would prioritize and assign owners to the issues requiring action.

We conducted a trial Gemba walk and asked technicians what they thought. They were extremely positive. They told us it was more helpful to them than the prior approach. Their feedback confirmed we were on the right track.

We finalized all details that evening. The next morning, we conducted the new Gemba walk and uncovered many issues holding back the performance and safety of the plant. Engagement, safety, and productivity improved almost immediately. It stayed that way for a long time.

Less than Success Stories

There are many examples of how Layered Audits prevent or expose problems. The next story illustrates how an engaging Layered Audit could have prevented many years of problems.

Go See for Yourself

My Kaizen team was focused on reducing changeover time for a painting operation at an Oregon ceiling tile plant. After reviewing changeover reduction techniques, we watched a changeover in progress.

A technician was spraying the front of the paint booth with water in order to remove the paint from the earlier production run. Afterwards, she walked behind the booth. After three minutes, she returned to complete her work at the front of the paint booth. None of the team members followed her to the back of the booth.

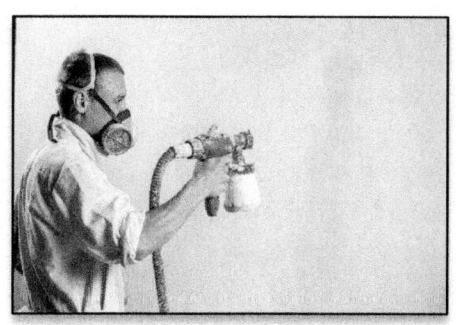

After the changeover was complete, we asked her to show us what she had been doing in the back of the paint booth. To our horror, she had to squeeze between a post and a wall, make her way to the paint tanks, stand on a natural gas line, twist her body, and reach above her head to open a valve. Was it always done this way? She told us it had been that way since the plant opened sixteen years before.

An immediate change was needed. The equipment was too difficult to relocate in the short time we had during the Kaizen. We knew we had to sell the idea to the leadership team and demonstrate the safety and financial justification for the change.

Luckily for us, the paint system was designed with limited automation capabilities. We didn't have to relocate the tanks or make major modifications. We determined that automating the valves on the paint tanks would eliminate the need for paint technicians to put themselves at risk in the back of the paint booth. We had an electrical engineer on the team. While we worked on other aspects of changeover time reduction, he developed cost estimates for paint tank valve automation.

Normally, engineers do research and build estimates with a high degree of accuracy prior to presenting their findings. In the spirit of Kaizen, he put together a cost estimate with high confidence the same day. Now we had to sell our idea to the leadership team.

During the remainder of the Kaizen, we simplified procedures, enhanced accessibility of tools, and improved the overall coordination of work during the changeover. We reduced changeover time by more than 50 percent and accomplished our objective.

Ten leadership team members joined us for the report out. We thanked them for attending and explained the improvements. We invited them to walk with us through the new changeover procedure.

We started in the front of the paint booth and demonstrated the first steps. Next, we walked to the back of the booth. One by one, leadership team members ascended and descended stairs that crossed over the line to get to the back of the booth. They squeezed past the post and wall. We demonstrated the effort to open and close paint tank valves.

From the looks on the faces of the leadership team, they were unaware of what had been happening in the back of the booth for the past sixteen years. The Plant Manager said, "we need to automate these valves immediately." Right on cue, our electrical engineer presented the cost estimate and received approval.

Within three months, valves were automated and the sixteen-year problem was corrected. If someone had conducted Layered Audits during construction of the plant, the problem would have been avoided. The best way to understand what's going on is to go see for yourself.

Layered Audits at Home or in the Office

I've told many stories about manufacturing and testing spaces. Kaizen isn't limited to those applications. During my time as Lean Champion, we ran many Kaizen events in office areas. One of these areas was the Capital Project Document Storage room.

After decades of completing capital projects all over the world, we had forty-four file cabinets scattered throughout the building, with project files that might be referenced anywhere from frequently to never. Company policy was all capital project files had to be retained and stored, regardless of age or relevance. There were so many files, it was almost impossible to keep track of everything.

Luckily, we had someone whose chief responsibility was the management of these files. I have no idea how Jessica kept up with them. When she was on vacation, it was a nightmare for the Capital engineers to find the files when they were needed. Jessica admitted that she received many frantic calls from engineers when she was away from the office or on vacation.

We chartered a Kaizen event focused on simplifying the Capital Project file system. With Jessica as the Team Leader, she chose a team of enthusiastic Capital Engineers to help her organize and make sense of things.

After three days, the difference was startling. No longer were there forty-four file cabinets all over the place. Now, there were *twenty-two* in a room that had been a utility closet. Every cabinet was logically organized and visibly labeled. It used to take hours to find files. If Jessica was out of the office, it could take days. Now, any file could be found in less than three minutes.

The team built a workstation for short-term file use. They designed a sign-out sheet for longer-term needs. Lighting was improved and the walls were painted to brighten up the space. The team created a two-minute audit for Jessica to conduct on a daily basis (Layer 1). Weekly, a Capital manager audited the total system to make sure people were following the rules (Layer 2). Bi-weekly, leadership audited the space as part of the Global Technology Gemba walk (Layer 3).

Then, Jessica took a vacation and no one had to bother her. That's great news. Layered Audits reinforced the value of the new file system. The Capital Engineering team followed the rules as designed. From then on, anyone could find files any time they needed them. And Jessica could finally relax, at least a little bit.

How to Develop Effective Layered Audits

Define the purpose of the audit

- Why do you want to audit?
- What benefit are you trying to create?
- What behaviors are you trying to reinforce?
- Can you define the purpose in a way people will want to participate and engage?

You made critical changes and identified Clear Benefits (spoke 5). You want to make sure everyone receives the benefits at all times. Define the purpose of the audit to reinforce those benefits. This is an example of an audit purpose statement:

To drive ownership of the Lock out Tag out process through the organization in a way that reinforces importance, identifies opportunities for improvement, closes any gaps, and develops discipline to the process for the protection of all employees.

Develop a clear purpose people can easily understand and relate to. Design the audit to achieve the purpose.

Identify areas to audit

It would be easy to try to audit everything to support the purpose. Resist the temptation and pick the most critical areas. Where should you look or engage to assure the purpose is achieved? If there are many areas to audit, consider separating them into different audits. Schedule different times, days, or auditors. Rotate areas and responsibilities.

Identify elements to audit

The audit assesses the health of the system. Identify the elements that represent system health. You should be able to get a sense for how things are operating by reviewing random elements at random times. If someone is not following a critical procedure on Tuesday and makes an excuse for it, observe someone else on Thursday working with a different procedure. If they're not compliant, you have a systemic problem.

Create metrics and look for trends in performance

Develop ways to score the audit and identify performance trends. Is the system improving or deteriorating? Scoring doesn't have to be complicated. It can be a point system or counts of yes or no answers. Take emotion or subjectivity out of the rating system, if possible.

Build engagement and visibility

People need to know you care about what they're doing. The audit reinforces this through engagement. Rather than asking yes or no questions, design an audit requiring questions to be answered through discussions with and demonstrations by those who do the work. Use *"show me"* questions. They will enhance understanding, support, and Recognition (spoke 8) of the importance of the system. The questions show your interest. The answers demonstrate knowledge and discipline to the system. Learn and improve together.

While engagement is critical at the individual level, you'll also want others to know you have invested time and effort to audit. Create Visible Evidence (spoke 3) of the audit. Use sign-offs, dates, measures, Status Indicators, or other ways to show you were there and what you found. Post results in a visible location, in close proximity to where the work was audited.

Simplify the audit

The audit should take no more than five minutes. People are busy and don't have time for a lengthy audit. When you engage with someone, it will add time. Five minutes forces you to review the most important elements. Stay focused. The goal is achievable.

Document the audit

We should be informally auditing systems continuously. Leadership demonstrates their commitment by doing so. But, there's no way for the organization to know your findings until you document and post them for everyone to see.

Define the layers

Who should be auditing and with what frequency? Define responsibilities and frequencies. Require sign-offs or other Visible Evidence of participation.

Everyone can be an auditor

You don't have to be an expert to audit. Sometimes it's better if you're not. You'll be required to engage with those doing the work. Seek to understand what's going on and if help is needed.

Rotate auditors through the organization. Different perspectives expose additional opportunities and issues to be corrected or improved. The Maintenance Supervisor can audit administrative offices as easily as the Office Manager can audit the manufacturing floor. Empower the organization to participate.

Commit to help, not blame

When something doesn't look right during an audit, help resolve the issue immediately. Don't blame others. Seek to understand what's in the way of doing things right. Help them do things properly. It's a commitment of time and effort. Changes improve safety, productivity, and other critical results. Your help will support and sustain those improvements.

You can't ignore deviations from standard. You must be willing to lend a hand to help and correct the behavior leading to increased safety risk or poor performance (Accountability). If you don't, it's like saying it's okay to do the wrong thing. Imagine you observe someone who isn't following a required safety procedure, such as Lock out Tag out, or Confined Space entry. You have a duty of care to keep them safe. If you don't deal with the issue immediately, you aren't taking your duty seriously and you may be liable for injury or damage to property.

Mistakes to Avoid

Not committing the time to audit

If you think the improvements will be sustained without engagement and intervention, you're fooling yourself. One way to let the changes go back to the original condition is to stop auditing. People will think you don't care and will stop caring as well.

Not engaging

If you audit from afar, you won't see what's actually happening. You won't be trusted. Two-way learning will be lost. All you will be doing is checking a box. People will know that you don't care enough to help them.

Assigning blame

When you see someone doing something incorrectly, it's easy to blame the person, not the process. Most people don't do things wrong on purpose. If you assign blame, it won't take long for the system to degrade and for people to justify your blame. They may scatter when they see you coming.

Making the audit complicated or time consuming

If the audit takes too long, people will come up with reasons not to participate. If it's difficult to conduct, it may not be done properly. People will have a hard time auditing effectively. Focus on the system and the people doing the work, not on complex audit requirements.

Checking the boxes

Sometimes you just want to avoid auditing. It was created to reinforce critical changes or elements of work that must be followed. If you check the boxes without understanding or engaging with the system, you may overlook something critical. If you do and sign off, it's like saying it's okay to work improperly. This is worse than skipping the audit entirely.

How Leadership Commitment Supports Layered Audits

Leaders allocate time to conduct audits. They participate in Layered Audits at the defined frequency. They look for evidence of audits being conducted. They engage. Leaders pay attention to the results and interactions that arise.

Leadership Commitment is demonstrated when there is more than a passing knowledge of the system being audited. Engagement drives learning. Leaders are open and willing to learn. When there is a deviation from standard, they seek to understand the reasons and offer help to rectify the situation. If they don't know how to solve the problem, they ask for help. If someone still chooses to ignore or misapply the standard, they hold themselves accountable to redirect to the desired behavior.

Don't back off Layered Audits at the defined frequency, unless the organization improves them or puts something in their place. Layered Audits protect the system. They reduce the risk of returning to less effective behaviors and performance.

Summary

Layered Audits are the first line of defense for implemented changes. Although the organization has been notified, trained, and has everything they need to do their work in the safest, most productive manner, some will not immediately behave as expected. Use Layered Audits as your opportunity to verify, engage, and correct the behavior that deviates from the new standard.

Over time, it might feel like the organization has "*won*" and Layered Audits are no longer needed. This feeling usually happens one to two years after a change. The natural reaction is to reduce or eliminate audits. This is the time to recommit. The organization is watching to see if the changes are still critical. Your help is still needed. Layered Audits are your way of showing you are there to help every single day.

You don't have to conduct Layered Audits the same way every time. Randomize the elements and the order. Engage with someone you haven't spoken with in a long time. Teach someone new how to effectively conduct the audit. Make it interesting and engaging. Identify three things that could be improved or reinforced every time you audit.

The next two spokes (Accountability and Recognition) are focused on the behaviors required to sustain critical changes and results. What do you do when you see someone or something that deviates from standard? Accountability, the seventh spoke on the Wheel of Sustainability, provides the answer.

Layered Audits Takeaways:

How strong Leadership Commitment supports Layered Audits:

How weak Leadership Commitment damages Layered Audits:

What I can do to improve my approach to Layered Audits:

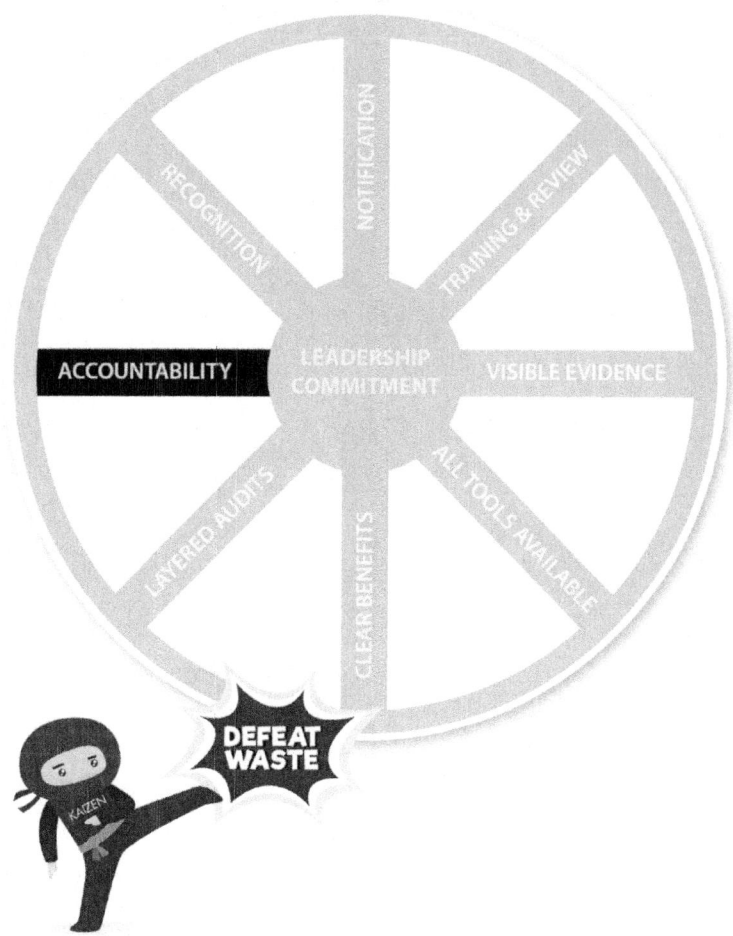

CHAPTER 8

ACCOUNTABILITY

When there is a deviation from standard, leaders demonstrate their Accountability by immediately stepping in to understand why, offering help, and correcting the situation and behavior.

Introduction

The word Accountability gets used a lot. We are accountable for our actions. I hold myself accountable to write this book. In the context of the Wheel of Sustainability, Accountability must be created for the implemented critical changes.

Imagine your team has implemented a solution to a critical business problem. Leadership has notified the organization of the changes (spoke 1). The team has delivered Training and Review (spoke 2). Changes are visible and it's almost impossible to do things wrong (spoke 3). Necessary tools were provided to accomplish the work safely and effectively (spoke

4). Clear Benefits were confirmed (spoke 5). Layered Audits are in place to verify the changes are understood (spoke 6).

Now imagine people don't follow the changes as designed. How is this possible? What can your team do? Fire everyone? Possibly, but there is something deeper than resistance and anarchy going on. What could it be?

The answer is Leadership hasn't demonstrated Accountability for the changes. Because of this, the organization doesn't understand the importance of the changes or take them seriously.

Here's an example of Accountability: You're walking to a meeting. You'll get there on time if you walk fast. On the way, you see someone about to do something that will likely cause an injury. What do you do? Avoid the issue and keep walking? Of course not. You step in and stop the person from doing something dangerous. You want to create this level of Accountability in your organization.

Don't turn a blind eye to someone not doing what's right. If you do, you are saying that doing the wrong thing is acceptable. When faced with a risky or critical deviation from standard, step in and help correct the situation.

The approach to correcting unsafe and unproductive behaviors matters. If you saw a small child about to touch a hot stove, you'd drop what you're doing, run to the child, and pull their hand away. You might yell to get their attention. Some of us would keep yelling. Others calmly explain why touching a stove is a *no-no*. A calm, caring, and instructive approach may prevent an injury and tears.

Because we're not dealing with children who do what we say (*maybe*) and don't want to disappoint us (*also maybe*), leaders must consider how to approach someone who isn't following the standard. Start with possible reasons for the behavior:

- They don't realize they aren't following the standard.
- They forgot the correct procedure.
- They're distracted.
- They were encouraged to do things differently.
- They think their way is better than the standard.

When you engage, reinforce the changes in a positive and supportive way. Explain *why*, not just *what*. Listen to their reasons. Then, just like dealing with someone who is about to do something that will cause injury, be firm in your convictions to follow the standard. Deviations are unacceptable.

Take the time to confirm understanding and how you can help them to do things in the right way. Even if they believe they have a better way, don't waver. Support the standard.

If they want to make a change, it must be reviewed by the team or another group. They can decide to act on the suggestion. Don't make a change unilaterally. There is an exception:

The change creates a hazard that was not identified prior to implementation.

In this case, create a temporary work-around and provide immediate feedback to the team. Revise the standard using all spokes of the Wheel of Sustainability.

Principles of Accountability

- Leaders take personal responsibility to correct deviations from standard.
- Nothing is more important than working in the safest, simplest, and most productive way. Anything else is unacceptable.
- When someone deviates from standard, immediately provide help and correct the behavior

Success Stories

Let's See How Things Go

At the beginning of my tenure as Oregon ceiling tile plant Production Manager, we were performing below budget commitments. There were many reasons, but most issues were related to our approach to standard work and changeovers. I knew I could make a quick impact, and implemented strict rules around changeovers:

- No one is allowed in the break room during a changeover without Team Manager approval.
- Everyone must be available to help during the changeover.
- When the line is ready to start up, all technicians must be at their workstations.
- *"One Best Way"* changeover procedures (which were developed by the technicians) must be followed to the letter. No exceptions.

Changeovers were the most critical activity during the production run, I explained. In order to execute the safest, most efficient changeover possible, everyone had to participate and help. It couldn't be done from the break room.

Technicians didn't like the *"no breaks during changeover"* rule. They thought it would limit their ability to get their breaks during their shift. I believed improved changeover performance would increase break scheduling flexibility.

Employees came to my office to express their displeasure. After listening to their point of view, I explained why I felt the rules were necessary. The plant had a culture of teamwork. There was no way to help from the break room. I told them, *"let's give the new rules a chance and see how things go."* I was firm in my convictions. They didn't like my answer.

At the start of every changeover, I walked to the break room to ensure people were following the rules. I didn't want to put all of the burden on the Team Managers. I felt accountable for rule enforcement. Whenever I found people in the break room, I asked if their Team Manager had approved the break. Most of the time, they indicated they hadn't by returning to the line.

After four weeks, average changeover time dropped by one-third and was more predictable. Technicians noticed the results. Visits to my office by *"dissatisfied customers"* became less frequent.

Team Managers became more comfortable enforcing the changeover rules. They knew I had their back and they were seeing results. They demonstrated Accountability and took ownership. It was no longer *"Adam's rules"*.

Changeovers became a source of pride in the plant. Teamwork strengthened and performance improved. What was once difficult and frustrating, was now safe, simple, and predictable. Most importantly, no one ever missed their breaks.

The Five Whys

The Five Whys is a method that can be used to understand why a change isn't being followed. It helps you get to the root cause of any resistance or problem you observe. If you find someone doing something in a non-standard manner, ask *why* until you get to their motivation for doing it differently. It may take five or more *whys*. It could take less. Here's a sample conversation:

Sue (Joe's manager): "I notice you're adjusting the equipment differently than the new procedure. Can you tell me *why* you are doing it this way?"

Joe: "From my many years of experience, I have found that it's better to adjust the equipment in the order I'm doing it."

Sue: "I know you think it's better. Can you tell me *why* you think it is?"

Joe: "It's the most comfortable and stress-free approach I know."

Sue: "It can be uncomfortable doing something differently and it takes time to get used to something new. Can you tell me *why* you're more comfortable doing it the old way?"

Joe: "It doesn't make sense to do step 3 after step 2. Step 3 should come after step 4."

Sue: "*Why* do you think step 3 should follow step 4?"

Joe: "If I do it my way, I don't have to search for the wrench when I get to step 3. I took it out of my tool box and used it when I did step 4. Then I can carry it to do step 3."

Sue: "Are you aware the team mounted required tools at each step? You don't have to carry them with you anymore."

Joe: "I didn't know that. I guess I forgot."

Sue: "Let me show you. See, the tools are right where you need them for each step."

Joe: "I can't believe I missed that. Thanks for showing me."

Sue: "You're welcome. Now that you know, I need you to follow the prescribed order. When you do, please let me know what you think."

Joe: "I'll give it a try and let you know how it goes."

In this case, it took four *whys* to uncover the root cause of the issue. What else happened? Sue listened to Joe. She helped him understand the proper procedure. She reinforced the requirement to follow it, identified the benefits, and made the commitment to get his feedback.

Sue demonstrated Accountability. Joe is likely to do the right thing from now on and may communicate what happened to his co-workers. Holding yourself accountable is not always easy and can be time consuming, but the benefits outweigh the effort. The next story describes how Accountability was established in a testing facility.

Ownership at the Right Level

I supported teams of technicians, scientists, engineers, project managers, and leadership across four Value Streams during the last six years of my corporate career. Teams developed and launched new products, deployed capital equipment, and built and supported factories around the world. All Value Streams had access to the Pilot Plant to support their efforts.

The Pilot Plant was a series of disconnected processes with resources and capabilities to test new materials, products, processes, and other ideas in a controlled way. Information gleaned from tests and trials was utilized in the delivery of projects, and product and process development. Every area in the Pilot Plant had an Area Owner, responsible for scheduling, care, performance, and safety of their area.

Area	Owner	Audit Date	Compliant?
Testing Lab #1	Mary J.	June 15	○
File Room	Jessica D.	June 4	○
Paint Line	Eddie C.		●
Equalizer	Steve M.	June 28	○
Packaging	Angela R.	June 19	○
Shipping	Dean Y.	June 21	○
Wood Shop	Troy B.	June 7	○

Most Area Owners were technicians. They scheduled their areas to allow them to be utilized effectively and keep wait times to a minimum. They were proud of their equipment and took their responsibilities seriously.

I spent many hours in the Pilot Plant, in support of the Area Owners. It was a critical resource. In my early days as Lean Champion I met Roy. Recently named Pilot Plant Leader, he was responsible for overall Pilot Plant performance and safety. He worked in one of our factories prior to his arrival at the Corporate Center. He had vast equipment knowledge and limited leadership experience.

Roy was also an Area Owner and participated in the annual Pilot Plant cleanup. This was a multi-day effort at the end of the year. It required full participation by the technicians. They'd review all materials, supplies, and equipment throughout the Pilot Plant, clean out the clutter, and organize things in as safe and productive manner as possible. There was no time for other work. All development and testing stopped during this time.

Technicians **HATED** the annual cleanup. They knew it wouldn't take long for things to go back to the way they were. Roy expressed his irritation to me many times as an Area Owner. Once he became Pilot Plant Leader, he made it his mission to eliminate the annual cleanup.

I encouraged Roy to discuss the situation with his manager and gauge his support. He did and was disappointed. His manager was supportive, but didn't offer solutions Roy thought he could implement on his own. He wanted his manager to demand everyone clean up after themselves.

Over the next few months, we facilitated a number of 5S Kaizen events in the Pilot Plant. Areas were made safer and more productive. Area Owners who had completed 5S events implemented managing systems that kept their areas in top shape.

Other areas didn't have the same systems. They were cluttered and disorganized. Roy was reaching his boiling point. One morning, following the weekly Pilot Plant Technician huddle, he stopped me on the way to my office.

Roy: "I've had it. My manager won't hold everyone accountable to keep the Pilot Plant organized and safe. He says it's our responsibility, but doesn't do anything when people aren't compliant. What can I do?"

Me: "I want to help you, but first I need to ask you an important question: Who's the Pilot Plant Leader?"

Roy: "I am. You know that."

Me: "I do, but I wanted to make sure that you do. You set expectations and hold Accountability. You are like the Operations Manager. Your boss is the Plant Manager. The Plant Manager needs you to get *your* operations in order."

Roy: "I don't know how to do that. What do you suggest?"

Me: "I have some ideas. Let's figure this out together."

Over the next two weeks, we developed our strategy for the Pilot Plant:

- Set clear safety and organization expectations for all areas.
- Define responsibilities for all Area Owners (not just the 5S Area Owners).
- Prioritize and schedule areas to implement 5S.
- Implement a weekly Gemba walk.
- Create a visible Area Owner Accountability system.

We installed a four-foot by six-foot white board in the Pilot Plant meeting room and put lines and names on it. We were ready to explain it at the next Pilot Plant huddle.

Roy introduced the strategy for making the Pilot Plant safer and more productive. Technicians listened with keen interest and asked many questions as he described the changes. They felt they'd be able to meet the new requirements, but were skeptical there would be any change in behavior of others who used the Pilot Plant.

Then Roy explained the Area Owner board. On it were thirty Pilot Plant locations with the corresponding name of the Area Owner and a space to write a date. At the beginning of the month, a red magnet would be placed at each location, signaling requirements weren't yet met. Once compliance was achieved, the Area Owner would replace red with a green magnet and write the date. The following month, all magnets were to be set back to red.

The technicians were *furious*. They thought red magnets made them look like they weren't doing a good job. Sensing a coup, I explained the board was a visual and urgent way to identify areas that needed help to be compliant. The system wasn't a reflection of the specific Area Owners, unless they hadn't made an effort to meet monthly requirements or didn't ask for help. I believed we'd be able to eliminate the **HATED** annual cleanup if we achieved monthly compliance in all areas.

At this point, the technicians started to buy in and support the idea. They were skeptical everyone would be motivated to get to green every month. I decided to provide an incentive. "The first month we achieve 100 percent compliance, I'll buy everyone lunch." That got their attention.

Roy described the new weekly Gemba walk. We'd invite managers of those who used the Pilot Plant and tour all 5S areas. We'd look for issues to correct and ways to reinforce compliance to requirements. We'd sign off and post findings to demonstrate our Accountability.

I attended every huddle and reinforced the new systems for the next three months. I encouraged technicians to get their areas to green before the end of the month. After two months, we hadn't achieved 100 percent compliance.

With two days left in the third month of the *"Area Owner Challenge"*, there was one technician whose area was still red. The technicians pressured Eddie to meet the requirements and make sure I would buy them lunch. They were nice about it, but they were serious. Our system of Accountability was finally working. We achieved our compliance goal.

I invited managers to the recognition lunch. Conversations centered around family and sports. Every so often, people mentioned how much nicer the Pilot Plant was to work in. Technicians teased Eddie for almost preventing the lunch from happening. The small investment was paid back many times over.

Month after month we stayed 100 percent compliant. By the end of the year, the **HATED** annual cleanup was eliminated. Pride in the facility grew. In the following years, the Pilot Plant was benchmarked many times for the strong Accountability, ownership, and systems driving new products and projects to be delivered in the safest and most productive way possible.

The next story is about an Area Owner who took it upon himself to solve a problem and create Accountability for everyone who used his area. Once again, it comes from the Pilot Plant.

Color-Coded Badges

The Pilot Plant was filled with operating and testing equipment. Technicians, engineers, and scientists used it to try out their ideas and experiment to create new processes and products. The Wood shop was the most active area in the Pilot Plant.

Mel was the Area Owner. He managed a tight ship. As most of the equipment in the Wood shop had cutting and grinding capabilities, there was a need to train people to use the equipment safely and properly.

Mel took his responsibilities seriously. He trained and qualified anyone who wanted to operate the equipment. No one was allowed to use the equipment who wasn't trained and qualified personally by him. A few unqualified employees used the equipment and word got back to Mel. He wasn't happy about it.

He knew he needed to do something to keep people safe and doing the right thing at all times. He confronted the rule breakers and didn't get the desired results. Then, he spoke with their managers. That didn't work either. One day, he looked like he was about to blow a gasket.

Mel: "I'm sick of this. People should act like adults and follow the rules."

Me: "You're right, they should act responsibly. What do you want to do about the rule breakers?"

Mel: "Fire the lot of them!"

Me: "Okay, I understand your pain. You know we can't fire everyone who breaks the rules. If we did, we'd run out of people. Are you willing to try something else?"

Mel: "Not really, but I guess I don't have a choice. We can't let people use the equipment they're not qualified for. One of these days, someone's going to get hurt."

Me: "There must be something we can do to strengthen compliance. We need to take the burden off you and hold people accountable."

Mel: "Look, I train and qualify more than one hundred people every year. I track who I've trained and verify compliance as much as I can. I can't be everywhere. What do you suggest?"

Me: "Let's say I see Judy using the band saw. I have no way of knowing if she's been trained and qualified. I can ask her, but she may not want to tell me. Do you think there's a way to enforce compliance that isn't dependent on you?"

Mel looked at me kind of funny – I get that look often. He was processing my question.

Me: "There's one spot in the Wood shop I can assess compliance any time. Do you know where that is?"

Mel: "I know, it's the tool board."

Me: "Right. You've made it easy. It's almost impossible to do things incorrectly. Everyone knows their responsibility and Accountability. No tools go missing or get left around the shop."

Just then, the light bulb turned on. I could tell Mel wanted to figure things out for himself.

Three weeks later, Mel was ready to share his solution. He created a badge system with three colors: red, blue, and yellow. Yellow indicated low safety risk, blue was moderate, and red was high. He reviewed each of the fifty pieces of equipment in use in the Wood shop, determined risk levels, and attached the appropriate colored badges.

Mel communicated the new system to the organization. He assigned badges to employees based on their training and skills he personally observed and qualified. No one could use equipment unless they had a badge indicating the required risk level or higher. Only Mel could issue higher risk-level badges.

We were now able to help Mel keep everyone safe. He put in all of the preparation and effort. The rest of us helped ensure compliance. We stopped hearing stories of people breaking the rules in the Wood shop. And for good reason. Leaders held themselves accountable to help Mel keep the area safe. The rest of the organization stayed compliant. It was that way through my last days at the company. Knowing Mel, they still are.

In this next story, Accountability helped us find the root cause of a problem causing excessive scrap and downtime.

Trust but Verify

I was part of a team assigned to improve performance at a ceiling tile plant in Alabama. The plant lost money many months in a row. We were tasked with identifying and implementing improvements to drive performance to achieve the full year budget. We called the effort a "*Full Court Press,*" which meant we were 100 percent focused and wouldn't give up until we accomplished our mission.

The plant had one board forming line and two fabrication and packaging lines. The board forming line was clearly not the problem. Quality, productivity, and safety were well above budgeted rates. Losses came from the underperforming fabrication and packaging lines.

We attended the morning production meeting on the day we arrived. We introduced ourselves to the staff and reviewed performance. They welcomed us, but weren't sure we'd be able to deliver needed results in a short time.

Next, we toured the fabrication department and observed many problems. We spoke with operators, mechanics, and staff for their feedback and ideas. They were hopeful we could help them return to budget performance.

Each team member had a specialty. One was interested in the programming used to control the equipment. Another was focused on the coordination of materials and resources. My area of expertise was the flow of materials through the production line. During our tour, I noticed many shutdowns and jams. I knew I could help.

With the agreement of our team leader, another team member and I took a detailed look at the higher volume fabrication and packaging line. Walter was the Line Leader. He was interested in our observations and asked if he could walk with us. We were happy to have him along. He introduced us to the crew and lent credibility to our efforts. He appreciated our approach of watching the line carefully to identify the causes of line stops and jams.

We stopped at the press. It's critical for the boards to enter and exit the press squarely and on center, so that holes are punched properly. Guide rails on the lower surface of the press are used to maintain board location. After exiting the press, a gate stops the board and allows the press to punch the next one.

Something didn't look right. As boards exited the press, they struck the stop-gate at an angle. Cracks formed at the leading edge of each board.

We asked the Press Operator if he was concerned about the cracks. He said the edge damage was minimal, and it would be cut out later down the line. It looked as though the cracks were too deep to be removed completely. We took notes and walked on.

At the next stations, boards were painted and cut into tiles. Then, they passed through an inspection station. Two Quality Control Operators rejected one-third of the tiles that passed by. There was so much scrap, they couldn't keep up and stopped the line many times.

During some downtime, we asked about the scrap tiles they were rejecting. They showed us cracks that ran down the length of the tiles at an angle. They looked just like the cracks at the press. We asked for samples, which they gladly gave us.

We returned to the press and showed the tiles to the operator. He was shocked. He hadn't realized there was so much scrap. He immediately shut the line down to make adjustments.

I asked to look inside the press to identify the reason boards were striking the stop-gate at an angle. After locking out the press, I took a closer look and was amazed.

The guide rails in the press weren't straight as designed. They were curved like bananas. The *"banana"* rails caused the boards to turn at an angle in the press. As they left the press, the misalignment caused boards to strike the stop-gate at an angle and damaged their edges.

All other plants replaced press guide rails twice a year. It didn't look like the plant was following this schedule. I felt the Accountability to get this problem resolved.

Me: "At our Pennsylvania plant they replace press guide rails every six months. Do you follow a replacement schedule?"

Walter: "I doubt it. These rails have been in the press a long time."

Me: "Think back, if you can. When was the last time they were replaced?"

Walter: "Hard to say. Maybe two or three years."

Press Operator: "C'mon man, they probably haven't ever been replaced."

Me: "Do you have any backup rails in the storeroom?"

Walter: "I sure hope so. Let's go take a look."

We found a backup set of press guide rails. Fortunately, they were straight. We replaced the *banana* rails with straight ones, restarted the press, and immediately shut it off. This time, the boards were damaged at a different angle.

We quickly identified the problem. The stop-gate was angled for the *banana* rails and hadn't been adjusted for straight ones. Once it was set perpendicular to the straight rails, edge damage disappeared. After handshakes and high fives, we created a monthly audit and a six-month press guide rail replacement program.

During the week, the team made many other improvements that helped the plant return to budgeted performance. The lesson here is to trust your processes, but verify them on a regular basis. If you see something, use Accountability to resolve the issue.

Less than Success Story

If Everyone's Responsible, Nobody's Responsible

I visited a consumer goods factory in Pennsylvania. They were profitable, but concerned their ability to service customer orders was deteriorating. I met with plant leadership and took a Gemba walk through the distribution center.

They were proud of their efforts to apply 5S. I asked Angela, the Distribution Center Manager, how they used 5S to help them service their customers. She was unsure of my question, so I posed it in a different way:

Me: "What benefits do you get by using 5S?"

Angela: "It's cleaner in the distribution center than before we used 5S."

Me: "It does look clean. Well done. How does that help you?"

Angela: "We don't spend time cleaning up behind each other."

Me: "How do you ensure it stays clean?"

Angela: "I remind our employees to use 5S and clean up after themselves daily. Sometimes they need additional reminding."

Me: "Can you show me an example?"

We walked to a tool board. There were spaces for seven different tools. The shape of each was painted on the board. It was apparent where things were to be placed, except all tools weren't on the board. Only two of the seven were present.

Me: "Where are the other five tools?"

Angela: "I'm not sure. People are probably using them right now."

Me: "Can we take a look or is there someone we can ask to find out?"

Angela: "We should be able to ask anyone here. Everyone's responsible for keeping the tool boards filled."

Me: "I'd like to find out how that's working."

We found a distribution center employee and asked him if he knew where the missing tools were. He wasn't sure. We walked to four other tool boards. Freshly painted, all were missing tools. Without an owner for the boards, there was no Accountability to keep them filled and ready for use. This led to less than effective cleaning.

During the rest of our Gemba walk, we found many more examples of how the lack of Accountability kept performance at low levels. When everyone's responsible, nobody's responsible. Once we identified systemic lack of Accountability as the underlying cause of low customer service levels, Angela and I chartered a Kaizen event to resolve the situation.

Accountability at Home or in the Office

In the story, *"Ownership at the Right Level,"* I described the Area Owner board developed by the Pilot Plant team. One of the Area Owners was me.

I felt it was unfair to name others Area Owners if I was unwilling to be one. I had to demonstrate the principles of area ownership to the organization to guide them along our cultural transformation.

My area was the Kaizen Promotion Office (KPO). It was a meeting room where all Value Stream teams conducted their weekly huddles. It was also used for monthly Global Leadership team meetings and other critical events. It was stocked with the necessary tools, materials, and supplies for effective meetings and problem-solving efforts.

I conducted a 5S audit every Monday morning and made sure everything was as it was supposed to be. If I wasn't available, I asked for help from someone who was willing to do a thorough audit and not just go through the motions.

Sometimes I'd find papers left on tables or equipment out of place. Instead of cleaning up for the responsible parties, I made it my mission to follow up and correct the undesirable behavior.

I didn't want to sound petty or vindictive. I did want the organization to learn how critical it was to adhere to the standard. The room was designed to be the safest, most productive room possible for everyone to use. I explained that deviations from standard were creating a negative impact on others who used the KPO.

I wasn't always met with receptive or understanding ears, but I never gave up. I couldn't shirk my Accountability to the people who used the KPO. It was just as important as any other work space. Eventually, the organization got the message, and there were far fewer examples of issues found on Monday mornings.

The KPO became a showplace. It was benchmarked many times. Many critical company meetings were held there. Eventually, some Board of Director meetings used it. Before I left the company, I was approached to help design other meeting rooms, using Accountability principles.

How to Develop Effective Accountability

Engage immediately

Like a moth to the flame, go directly to the issue or problem you observe. Seek to understand and offer help to return to standard. Be aggressive, not conservative. If you see something, say something. Even if you misinterpreted the situation, you are trying to help the organization do the right thing.

Empower others to assess and correct problems

Encourage the organization to help at all times. Make it safe for others to assess the current situation. Teach simple problem-solving methods, such as the five *whys*. It's okay to be wrong. Promote learning and reflection for every engagement.

Know why, not just what

To have Accountability, you must understand *why* changes were made, not just *what* they are. You may engage with those who don't understand. Convey the reasoning behind the changes. Why do we think safety, productivity, customer service, or stress levels will be improved?

The person doing work their way may not realize the reasons to do it differently or understand the thinking behind the changes. If you say, "*It's because I said so,*" or "*the company says we must do it this way,*" you aren't demonstrating your Leadership Commitment and Accountability.

Understand how all of the spokes of the Wheel work together in support of the changes

People may have forgotten things were put in place to help them accomplish work in an easier and safer way. If you know the total system, you can help others realize how much thought and effort went into the changes. Point out the visuals, tools, benefits, training, and audits. Take the time to demonstrate the changes. You are further cementing your Accountability and Leadership Commitment.

Check for understanding

Ask the person doing the job to demonstrate their understanding of the new standard. This avoids the "*because I said so*" approach. It gives them the opportunity to ask questions. Be willing to spend additional time. Remember Training and Review (spoke 2). Use Tell, Show, and Do.

Reaffirm the changes and offer help

Before you leave, summarize the conversation, reaffirm your commitment, and offer help. I doubt there will be another time you see the same person doing things the wrong way. There's one more thing you need to do.

Beg for forgiveness

If you're late to your next appointment, explain what happened and why you were late. Do it in a non-disruptive way. You're not making excuses; you are showing your Accountability to the critical changes. Others need to understand you've made a choice. Your priorities demonstrate your Leadership Commitment. They may follow your lead the next time they encounter a deviation from standard.

Mistakes to Avoid

Looking the other way

When someone deviates from the standard, it's easy to avoid the engagement or confrontation that may occur when correcting the behavior. If you choose to look the other way, it's like saying it's acceptable to do things wrong or in an unsafe manner.

Assigning blame

When you see someone do something wrong, it's natural to blame them for the problem. If you do, they'll be less willing to share issues with you. They may hide from you. This isn't the way to build a culture of engagement and empowerment. It's not always someone else's fault. Sometimes you have to look in the mirror to reveal the responsible person.

Putting the burden on one person

If Accountability to follow the standard falls on one person, they won't have the benefit of support and help to ensure things operate properly and safely. They may get distracted or overwhelmed. The rest of the organization won't get the benefit of learning from and preventing problems.

Knowing what, not why

If you just know *what* someone is supposed to do without understanding *why* they should do it, you won't create Accountability and ownership for the changes. When you tell someone what they should do, without telling them why, it's akin to saying, *"Do this because I said so."* You won't build engagement, trust, and commitment that way.

How Leadership Commitment Supports Accountability

When leaders see something that doesn't look right, they engage immediately. They assess the situation, determine root cause, and offer help to prevent future problems. It's not someone else's responsibility. This is the way leaders demonstrate their Accountability.

When there are critical changes, leaders demonstrate their knowledge and help others stay committed. They know there will be resistance. Leaders know people will look to them to see how serious they are about the new standard. Their Accountability will be confirmed.

Strong leaders affirm their commitment prior to implementation. They must be willing to put aside other duties when they see something that doesn't look right. It's a commitment of time and test of their resolve.

Leaders have more than a passing knowledge of the system during their audits. The more they engage, the more they learn. When there is a deviation, leaders seek to understand and offer help to return to standard. If they don't know how, they ask for help. If someone chooses to ignore or misapply the standard, leaders hold themselves accountable to correct the situation and behavior.

Accountability builds trust. It takes a long time to build and a short time to lose. Be purposeful on the changes you intend to hold yourself and others accountable to. Be ever vigilant to monitor and ensure they are properly followed. It's a test of your Leadership Commitment.

Summary

Accountability works hand in hand with Layered Audits. Constantly audit systems as you do your work and travel from place to place. When you see deviations from standard (and you will), you have to be willing to immediately correct the situation. More than that, you reinforce the importance of the changes by taking the time to help others.

The higher up in the organization you are, the more people you influence as you demonstrate your Accountability. You shouldn't have to drop what you're doing very often. There are others who can help. If you engage properly, the organization will remember your efforts and your Accountability. They may even tell stories about the day you helped correct a critical problem.

The last spoke of the Wheel of Sustainability is Recognition. Spoiler alert: It's not about awarding prizes. It is about the stories that tie efforts together in a sustainable way. Read on to learn how Recognition strengthens organizational support.

Accountability Takeaways:

How strong Leadership Commitment supports Accountability:

How weak Leadership Commitment damages Accountability:

What I can do to improve my approach to Accountability:

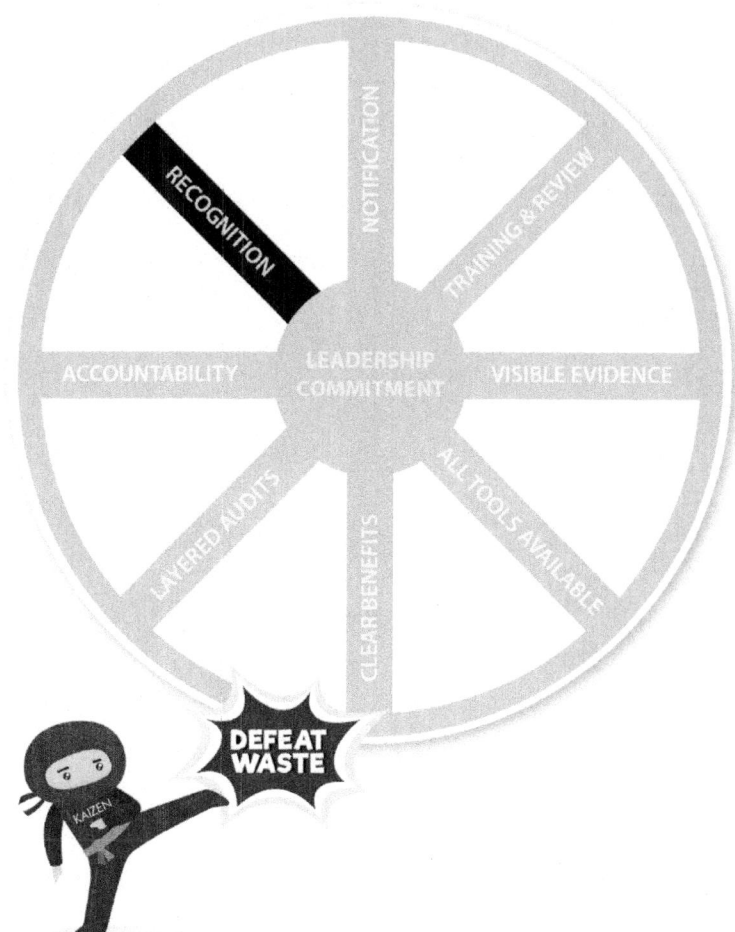

RECOGNITION

Recognition is built by sharing stories of success. Understanding cause and effect helps people make the connection between the changes and improved results, locking in their commitment.

Introduction

Many years ago, I won an award for helping my team improve scrap performance (Chapter 4 – *Beer is the Answer*). I received a check and a plaque with my name on it. I deposited the money in the bank and put the plaque on my wall. Every time I looked at it, I thought about what it represented. The money was gone quickly. The memory of the team and our achievement lived on.

Many people speak about Recognition in terms of awards and money. I think differently. Recognition represents the memory of the experiences resulting from something we do. It utilizes storytelling and leverages the understanding of cause and effect.

Until very recently in the vast expanse of history, knowledge was transferred orally through stories. Family histories were shared. We explained how things worked. Scientific phenomena were described. Other critical information was communicated from person to person. Village elders told their stories to an audience enthralled by their words. People passed those stories on to others.

Over time, we devised ways to record and print our stories. Now, we use computers and other advanced devices. We're trying to get the same effect. We tell stories to remember things, explain circumstances, and reinforce beliefs.

The eighth spoke of the Wheel of Sustainability is focused on the creation of stories that drive organization commitment to critical changes. Recognition highlights cause and effect. The intent is for the changes to be remembered, valued, and reinforced. In Chapter 5, I shared an example about long-handled wrenches positioned on both sides of a punch press. There was no need to search for tools, carry them, or worry about not having what was needed. They were right there. They helped people do their job. The work was safer, more efficient, and less of a pain in the neck.

Other were told about the wrenches. Their job got easier too. The *cause* was the wrench positioned near the press. The *effect* was an easier, simpler, and safer way to do work. Recognition happened when they told others about the wrenches at the press. It reinforced their commitment to use them, rather than the wrenches in their tool boxes.

Recognition is built using the Plan-Do-Check-Act (PDCA) cycle:

1. **Plan** the thing you are going to do – the changes you intend to make.
2. **Do** (implement) the changes. Note the cause.
3. **Check** the results of the changes. What was the effect you were trying to achieve?
4. **Act** to reinforce or improve the changes as necessary.

Repeat the PDCA cycle as many times as necessary to achieve the desired effect.

Recognition occurs between Do and Check. What did we do? What happened? Do we like the results? If not, decide how to Act. Learn and improve. Repeat the cycle until you achieve the desired results. Now, implement the changes.

Drive to achieve Recognition in the organization to strengthen sustainability. Start with those directly impacted by the changes. Then expand to those who support them. Finally, build Recognition in the total organization. You have achieved the ultimate Recognition when someone who wasn't involved in or affected by the changes tells its story to others. That's what winning looks like.

Principles of Recognition

- Commitment to the changes is strengthened by the telling of stories.
- When something positive happens, identify and communicate the cause and effect to promote buy-in.
- Use Recognition to drive additional improvement opportunities.
- Success stories are shared many times to enhance the culture of continuous improvement.
- When someone who wasn't directly involved in the changes shares a success story, it's a win.

Success Stories

Even the Most Organized Person Can Improve

In Chapter 8, I told the story of how we were able to eliminate the **HATED** annual Pilot Plant cleanup (*Ownership at the Right Level*). Working with the Pilot Plant Leader, we created a strategy to transform the facility. We implemented 5S across many areas. This is the story of the first 5S Kaizen and how we used it to create organizational Recognition and pull for additional 5S Kaizen events.

All areas of the Pilot Plant were candidates for improvement. They were in varying conditions of disorganization and clutter. We had to pick the first area strategically. If we could make sustainable improvements there, we could replicate our efforts elsewhere. Where should we start?

The *paint spraying area* was known for its organization and strong ownership. It was used by many scientists, technicians, and project team members. Improvements would impact many in the organization. It had a very strong Area Owner. Regina was known for her tenacity and ability to hold people accountable to follow the rules.

We asked Regina to lead the first Pilot Plant 5S team. She agreed, but wasn't sure what improvements were possible. She was proud of her area and had every right to be. I gave her a quick overview of the possibilities and advised her to pick team members. She immediately knew who to ask.

Over the next week, Regina visited with potential members and *strongly* encouraged them to join her team. Everyone said yes. How could they say no? She even convinced her manager to join. He raised quite a few eyebrows in his peer group. We were grateful for his Leadership Commitment.

The first day of the Kaizen was "*Sort*" day. We reviewed everything in the area and made tough decisions. We eliminated more than half of all parts, tools, equipment, and materials. Regina was shocked. She thought she had kept unused and unnecessary things out. She had been storing leftover materials and parts after testing was complete. Over time, they became hidden, damaged, or unusable.

We removed so much that we eliminated all of the highest storage locations. This allowed anyone to gather supplies or materials without using a step stool or reaching overhead. We added signs as a reminder that it was unacceptable to store anything above shoulder height.

The second day was "*Set in order*" day. We assessed everything that remained and identified ideal locations. We applied labels, painted outlines, and made it almost impossible to lose anything.

I overheard team members discussing repair parts for their paint guns. Each technician had their own *stash*. They didn't trust they'd be able to find what they needed otherwise.

I asked, "If we always knew where the repair parts were and they were immediately available, would you need to squirrel them away?" Team members agreed they wouldn't, but didn't yet trust 5S would keep things from being lost, stolen, or walking away.

"Let's figure out a way to keep that from happening," I said. We built and labeled storage bins for the parts, three feet from the spray booth.

They weren't willing to give up their *stash* yet. I asked them to use the storage bins first and hold others accountable to do so as well. After a month of success, they should donate their parts to the new bins. Their skepticism told me it would be a hard sell.

I assured them we were going to create a managing system and rules for the area. They would own the system and enforce the rules. Leadership was committed to support them. We'd teach them their role, starting with the report out. My responsibility was to coach the proper supporting behaviors. We had a member of the leadership team working with us. He agreed to champion our efforts.

We were now ready to Shine. We cleaned, inspected, repaired, and ensured everything was in optimal condition. Team members enjoyed this work. They repaired and replaced things that hadn't been working well for many years. Everything was done on the spot and at little cost. They were empowered to maintain things in top operating condition.

Next, we worked on managing systems to sustain all improvements. This included defining responsibilities for those using the area. We created Layered Audits, maintenance responsibilities, and a Gemba walk.

The team presented their results to a packed meeting room. There was much excitement, but nothing like what happened during the tour. Attendees were impressed at what the team had accomplished so quickly and the quality of the managing systems.

They were enthralled when Regina related the benefits of having repair parts available and not hoarded by technicians. She told a story of how she lost two hours looking for something a technician had locked in his desk. Because she didn't have the parts in her *stash*, she had to track him down, wait for his meeting to end, and then have him unlock his desk drawer. This was typical, not an exception. Now, because of 5S, she could get to anything she needed in seconds. This was an immediate improvement to productivity and safety. Recognition of cause and effect was strengthened.

At the end of the tour, there was much clapping and warm wishes for the team. Many attendees stayed to talk about 5S. The team recalled the same thought they had before the Kaizen event. "Regina's area is so organized. What improvement can we make?" Now they knew.

Regina's story continues. We used the Recognition of her improvement efforts to help others visualize what could be accomplished and created support for other Kaizen events. If Regina and I were with a group in the Pilot Plant, I'd ask her to give a tour of her area and explain the benefits of 5S. As she spoke, her pride came through and strengthened her Recognition.

The more I asked her to share her story, the more people asked her to show them her area. The momentum built up and it became a running joke. I'd walk up to Regina. Before I could say a word, she'd say, "Adam, who do you want me to tell the story to today?"

Regina had credibility as an Area Owner. She was the real-life example of the impact of continuous improvement. Soon, other Area Owners were using 5S, based on her success and the fact her area stayed organized, productive, and safe.

Over the years, most areas in the Pilot Plant used 5S and installed the same managing systems. These efforts helped the facility reduce safety risks, cut customer response time by more than 50 percent, and double productivity.

Eventually, people who didn't work with Regina were telling her story. This was the moment I realized Recognition was critical to sustainment. Improvement efforts took on a life of their own and didn't rely on a single person to drive them.

The Story of the Pink Tools Revisited

In Chapter 4, I told the story of the *pink tools* with an emphasis on Visible Evidence (spoke 3). This time, I'll highlight Recognition. If you recall, the team in Ohio decided the only way to keep tools from being lost or walking out of the factory was to paint them red. I coached Steve, the Plant Manager, how he should respond the first time the *Rules of the Tools* were violated. I suggested he raise such a fuss that the whole plant would notice.

Two months later, I returned to the plant to facilitate another Kaizen event. I learned there was one incident where tools had gone missing. People were telling stories about it. During a break, I visited with Steve to hear his perspective on the incident.

Me: "My Kaizen team is talking about something that happened recently. I understand you got involved when tools went missing on the line. Tell me what happened."

Steve: "I listened to your suggestion when you were here last time. To be honest, I thought you were full of it."

Me: "That's really not a revelation."

Steve: "That may be true. But, upon reflection, I realized you were just trying to help us sustain the results. By doing something unexpected, I could make a lasting impression on the team and the rest of the plant."

Me: "Okay, so what happened and what did you do?"

Steve: "Two weeks after the Kaizen, a screwdriver went missing. I raised some hell. Probably not as much as you were pushing for, but it seems to have done the trick. The tools haven't been misplaced since. Word has traveled all over the plant. The story has been retold many times."

The continued telling of the story of Steve raising hell created organizational Recognition for the *Rules of the Tools*. His Leadership Commitment helped sustain a positive result.

The next story illustrates how Recognition was used to hold me accountable.

Little Things Mean a Lot

A cat litter manufacturer experienced high levels of downtime, jams, and long changeovers on a critical production line. They invited me to their plant to observe the problem and identify opportunities for improvement. After reviewing performance, I joined the staff on a Gemba walk.

The line was running intermittently. We identified many opportunities to improve performance. Most notably, the filled boxes weren't flowing through the line consistently. We chartered a $4\frac{1}{2}$ day Reliability Kaizen event. The focus was to improve the flow of products through the line by centering, leveling, squaring, and balancing equipment.

In preparation, I had discussions with line operators, mechanics, and engineers, and made confirming observations. I reviewed my findings with Mike, the Plant Manager. It was apparent he didn't buy in to my approach. He had used a process called *"center-lining"*, with mixed results.

Center-lining, as he defined it, was a method engineers used to find the equipment's center and then balance everything on the line with respect to the identified center. It took weeks and didn't always solve flow problems. Engineers did the work. They didn't pass knowledge on to those running the line.

Locating and marking the center of the line is the first step in a Reliability Kaizen. Aligning, balancing, squaring, leveling, and optimizing product flow are the next steps taken to drive improved performance. Line operators and mechanics are critical team members. Reliability principles, techniques, and Recognition of cause and effect are transferred to the team members during the event. To lock in all changes, we install the Wheel of Sustainability before the end of the Kaizen.

I assured Mike that centering would be completed on the first day. We'd optimize all parts of the process in the following days. He was still skeptical, but heard enough, and gave his approval.

In most Kaizen events, I facilitate a structure and approach to the team charged with solving a problem. I rarely dictate specific actions. In a Reliability Kaizen, I direct all actions on the first day. Team members are given specific instructions. I do this because I've found my approach is new to most team members. On subsequent days, they identify, test, and implement their improvement ideas.

We kicked off with a review of Reliability principles. Next, we took a Gemba walk to the production line, shut it down, and locked it out. The first step was to identify the center of the carton wrapper. This is the part of the line where everything comes together – filled boxes of cat litter and shipping containers. I told the team everything leading up to it should be located and optimized to the center of the carton wrapper. They didn't think it was very important, at least not yet.

We located the center of the line at the midpoint of the conveyor frame on the exit side of the carton wrapper and secured a string to that point. Then, we pulled the string through the equipment, and identified the center of the conveyors leading up to the wrapper.

We found center along approximately one hundred feet of equipment and conveyor and pulled the string taut. Then, we marked center every four feet.

We removed the string and started the line back up. We observed the boxes of cat litter flowing to the carton wrapper. They were clearly off-center. The shipping container was as well. We could now easily see the twisting and turning of the boxes, which led to jams and downtime. Team members weren't expecting the problems to be so pronounced.

The next step was to level all of the conveyors leading up to and through the carton wrapper. Ideally, they should be no more than $\frac{1}{32}$" out of level at every *transition* (the point where one section of conveyor meets the next section). Using a *torpedo* level and some shims, we documented and corrected any conveyors that were out of level.

In the middle of the effort, I realized we needed something not available at the line. Having facilitated a team in the Weld shop (Chapter 7 – *Owning Their Solution in the Weld Shop*), I knew where to get it.

I walked to the shop and asked Sammy, the Area Owner, if I could borrow a 6-foot level. He reminded me of the *Rules of the Tools*: "Tools are on the tool board or in use, nowhere in-between. Return it as soon as you're finished." I assured him I would. I was aware of the rule, having helped the team develop it, after all. Sufficiently held accountable, I took the level with me.

The level was labeled: *"Weld Shop 6 Foot Level."* There was no way to not know where it came from and where it was supposed to go. Using it, we finished aligning and leveling the conveyors.

From time to time, I placed it on a table that was close to the line. A technician on the line reminded me to return the level to the Weld shop as soon as I was finished. Otherwise, Sammy would *"have my head"*. A supervisor from another line, who happened to be walking by, reiterated the message. Next, the HR manager told me about the *Rules of the Tools*. Finally, Mike, who was checking out our work, directed me to return the level to the Weld shop.

Were they messing with me? It didn't matter. What did matter was the story of Weld shop success and that the *Rules of the Tools* made it all the way through the plant. Recognition was strengthened every time I was reminded.

We completed leveling and started the line back up. Boxes of cat litter weren't twisting and turning, and ran more consistently than anyone remembered. We handed the line back to the production organization. And, yes, I returned the level to the Weld shop.

The next morning, we found out that the overnight shifts had run smoothly – much better than expected. The next step was to optimize the flow of the boxes with reference to the center of the line. This was easily done. The challenge was to ensure our new settings wouldn't change once the Kaizen was over.

We used lock collars, pins, and white labels to identify settings for all box sizes running on the line. Changeover steps were labeled in order with bright orange stickers. There was no way anyone would be able to overlook the Visible Evidence.

By the final day, line performance was significantly better. Line technicians thanked the team for correcting years of problems.

At the report out, team members remarked they were surprised how small changes impacted performance. Mike reinforced Recognition for the Reliability Kaizen by stating it should be applied to all other lines in the factory.

Recognize the Effort, Not the Results

In Kaizen events, team members are given the freedom to choose their own solution path. The choices and results aren't always what's expected. Long ago, I learned not to predict what a team was going to do. Their creativity and enthusiasm led them to solutions that beat my expectations.

I redirected my focus to helping teams accomplish as much as possible during the short time of the Kaizen event. I came up with creative ways to encourage progress. Some were silly and some were serious. Regardless, team members remembered the Recognition. These are some examples:

Clapping – I set milestones. When reached, I encourage team members to clap in Recognition. A sub-team returns with a plan for the next steps of their project. They review it with the rest of the team and then receive feedback on their approach.

At the end of the review, I'll say, "Let's show them how we feel about their efforts so far." Or, "let's show them some love." I clap and the rest of the team joins in. Those reviewing their plans start clapping too. There's usually pride in their faces. The more clapping, the more natural it becomes. Sometimes we make fun of ourselves for clapping, but we don't stop. It's infectious.

Being a source of energy – On the first morning of a Kaizen event, I shout out "*GOOD MORNING!*" Team members who don't know me wonder what's going on. Undeterred, I give it another try, "*GOOOOOOD MORNING!!*" Now, they get the point and some put out energy as they answer "Good Morning". On the third try, they're yelling at me. On the second morning, I bounce into the room, shouting "*GOOD MORNING!*"

and normally get the desired response on the first try. If not, there's always a second or third try. Once team members loosen up, they recognize that this is *their* Kaizen event, not mine. Recently, the Plant Manager used this approach as he greeted our Kaizen team on the second day. It was a nice surprise.

<u>Creating accountability</u> – Ground rules are used to keep the team focused and show respect for each other. These are some ground rules I've used all over the world:

- Be on time.
- Work hard and work together.
- No computers or cell phones.
- Be creative and challenge the status quo.
- Have fun.
- Be part of the solution.

In the Ohio ceiling tile plant, if you broke a ground rule, you were accountable to sing one of four songs:

1. The Itsy-Bitsy Spider
2. The Wheels on the Bus
3. Old McDonald Had a Farm
4. Stairway to Heaven

After a while, we'd prank someone to make them late and hear them sing. One team member brought his trombone and played Stairway to Heaven. It was awesome.

In China, team members who broke ground rules had to contribute ten yuan (Chinese currency) to a party fund. Local team members tried to convince American team members to contribute ten dollars if they broke ground rules. One dollar was worth six yuan. This wasn't equitable, but I can't blame them for trying to squeeze additional money out of the travelers.

Giving little trinkets – Earlier I told you money gets spent, but symbols of Recognition live on and remind us of our accomplishments and how we felt. Here's a story about the trinket I created:

I was always receiving shirts, hats, mugs, and other items that Sponsors gave team members in Recognition for their efforts. I wanted to do something special for my Kaizen team members. Eventually, I came up with the idea of creating a special coin, which I call my "*token of appreciation.*" It's gold colored. I give it to team members who make it through (survive) the full event. On the morning of the last day, I greet each team member as they enter the room, hand them a coin, shake their hand, and thank them for their participation.

Why did I pick a coin? I wanted to give people something that didn't take up much room and was unlikely to be thrown out. Have you ever thrown a coin away? I don't think I have, intentionally.

The first time I handed out coins, it felt uncomfortable. I didn't know how people would respond. I immediately received positive reactions and my discomfort quickly disappeared. Team members thanked me. Some asked me if the coins were chocolate or gold (they weren't). Most appreciated them. One team member said, "This is my new lucky coin!" I thought he was joking.

Three months later, I was walking through the same factory and heard a forklift driving near me. Stopping ten feet away, the driver called to me, "Adam, check it out. I still have my lucky coin!" I couldn't believe it. He was holding up his coin proudly. It really mattered to him. It made my day, and it still makes me smile when I think about it.

Nine months later, I was walking through the same factory, ran into the same team member, and he proudly showed how much his lucky coin had worn down. I'd been carrying a coin in my pocket since the first day I handed them out. He was pleased that his coin was more worn than mine.

I'd considered finding a new trinket to hand out to future team members. Now I realize there's no reason. People like the idea of the coin. It generates Recognition. The forklift driver clearly valued it and the memories of team success. If he showed it to me, he must have shown it to others. Recognition, even a *"lucky coin"*, drives commitment.

Each method of Recognition reinforces the value of the effort people put in to implement critical changes. When they look back at their work fondly, it builds support and commitment. When they tell the stories, others buy in.

Less than Success Story

The Vortex

Sometimes we don't see what's right in front of us. We just do what we do and deal with the problems that inevitably arise.

I facilitated a Kaizen event for a non-profit. Contributions were declining significantly. After taking a Gemba walk through the process, we identified the need to improve donor engagement. It was taking up to two months to acknowledge the highest value donations. No wonder donors were leaving in droves. Recognition was slow and not meaningful.

Two months before, I ran a workshop and donated the proceeds to Feeding America. I received a thank-you note less than thirty minutes after I sent my credit card payment. It felt good to be recognized so quickly.

We brought together a team and mapped out the donation acknowledgment process end to end. There were many points in the process where the information stalled. Of those, the worst was in the office of the VP of Finance. Information could sit in his office for weeks before anything happened. If he was busy with other duties, he might forget to take any action. A call from a disgruntled donor would restart the process.

It was so bad his office was nicknamed "*The Vortex*". Things came in and were lost to the world. This Recognition of poor performance had to be turned around.

The rest of the week, the team worked on ways to eliminate *The Vortex*. Time was reduced from two months to six days. Unfortunately, major damage had already been done to donor trust. It will take immense effort to reverse the negative Recognition for the organization.

Recognition at Home or in the Office

Recognition happens many places. Sometimes it's in a business setting, other times it's personal. This is a story of personal Recognition.

In my family, when one family member takes responsibility for something everyone else remembers someone else doing, we call that "*alternate history.*"

My mother was really good at creating *alternate history*. The thing is, we never argued about it, because it was always a fond memory. Why spoil her fun and Recognition of a story she treasured? Here's an example:

I met my wife on a blind date, well before the days of online dating. People actually knew someone they thought you might like going out with. I worked with her sister, who set us up. How could I say no? Our first date was fun and we got along very well. We dated for about a year and a half and people started to wonder if we would take our relationship to the next level and get married.

Peggy and I were happy to live independently. We never talked about marriage. We felt fortunate to be with someone we could be ourselves with and enjoy being around. We had many adventures we still talk about to this day.

My parents loved Peggy and made it clear they were happy we found each other. One day they were visiting me in North Carolina. My father, who didn't typically get too involved in my personal business, took me aside.

He was a man of few words, but I'll never forget what he said: "Can you imagine your life without Peggy?" I couldn't, and it wasn't many hours later when I proposed marriage. The words came out in the middle of the mulch aisle of a hardware store. We decided to not tell anyone until we had a few days to confirm we were serious.

Over the years, the story changed. My mother took credit for saying those words to me. She was so proud she was able to influence her son, the confirmed bachelor. Peggy and I laughed about it. We never corrected Mom. Dad didn't either. It didn't matter. Everyone was and is happy.

How to Develop Effective Recognition

Recognition is created through the telling of stories and connecting cause and effect. Build the elements and promote those stories using the cycle of Plan-Do-Check-Act (PDCA):

Understand the reason for the change (Plan)

Why did we think a change was needed? What was the problem we were trying to solve? What did we hope would happen? What was the evidence of the need for a change?

Identify the change that created the effect (Do)

What specifically was changed that impacted results? What did we do differently? What were we thinking and what were we hoping to have happen? Did it happen? Why did the change matter?

Identify the effect of the change (Check)

What was the result due to the change? What was the specific impact on safety, productivity, customer service, or any other critical business metric? What measure is being impacted? Can we make a case the change impacted the outcome?

Find specific, personal examples of how the change caused a better condition – tell stories (Check, Act)

Can someone in the organization point to something that happened to them that helped them personally? If so, what was it? How did it help them? Would they be willing to be the spokesperson for the positive results? Are they willing to share their story?

Create Visible Evidence of the change and the impact on the people and the organization (Check, Act)

Are there ways people walking by or into the area would know a change is creating a positive impact? Is there someone they can talk to about it? Is there an Area Owner? Is this person willing to show and demonstrate the change and how it creates a positive impact?

Identify an Area Owner (Act)

If you have an owner who cares about their area, they'll take pride in the changes that create positive improvements around safety, productivity, effort, and other measurable results. They are the "go-to" person. They have credibility. They can tell the stories for the organization.

Visit Area Owners (Act)

Conduct Layered Audits (spoke 6). Tour areas of change. Take Gemba walks. Meet with Area Owners. Help others visualize cause and effect. The more tours and participants, the better chance of them sharing the improvement stories as if they were on the team.

Say thank you (Act)

Recognize the efforts of those responsible and courageous enough to make changes. Don't reward them with money. Use that for other things. Make it easy and safe to be involved in the change process. People should feel good about their efforts. Saying *"Thank you"* is the simplest, cheapest, and possibly the most impactful Recognition of all.

Celebrate milestones (Act)

Don't wait for final results. Acknowledge progress along the way. Help teams celebrate the steps to the answer. Clap for them, give them a trinket. Take time out to thank them. Make it a big deal.

Celebrate failures (Act)

If you don't fail, you won't learn anything. The organization must not be afraid to fail. Celebrate when something unexpected happens. Encourage trial and error and learning cycles. Fail fast, fail often.

Mistakes to Avoid

Lacking awareness of the changes

People may not be aware changes have occurred. If you're not intimately familiar with the changes and their intended benefits, you won't be able to bring others' attention to them.

Not identifying cause and effect

If you don't recognize when something good happens due to a change that was made, others may not as well. Someone must be able to point out the positive benefits of a change. If not you, it may be no one.

Not measuring the effect of the change

You can't manage what you can't measure. If you don't measure the impact of a change, you won't know if positive or negative results are associated with it.

Not assigning an owner for the change

There needs to be a "go-to" person for all things related to the change. If there's no owner, there's no one to share the stories of the change. You can't say, "go see Lisa, she'll tell you all about it." Lisa will have no idea what you're talking about.

Punishing failure

Don't punish people when results don't meet expectations. If they tried, that's all you can ask for. If you punish failure, few people will volunteer for improvement efforts. That's what losing looks like.

How Leadership Commitment Supports Recognition

Leaders seek out positive outcomes and team effort. They share stories of them with the rest of the organization. They identify cause and effect. Once done, they promote the fact that the changes made a positive impact on the organization. They bring people's hearts and minds to the same conclusions. They tell stories of the changes in a positive and supportive way.

Leaders can influence the organization more than individual contributors. They can expand organizational awareness. What changes were made? Why were they made? What were the results? They expand the reach and opportunity to conduct additional improvement efforts.

Leaders cite specific examples of how the changes positively impacted the organization.

- Two hours of searching was reduced to two minutes.
- No one has been injured since we made the safety improvements.
- Our lead time from order to delivery is now two weeks, down from three months.
- The team worked together and never gave up, even when they experienced setbacks.

Thank people for their efforts. Even if things don't go as planned. Encourage people to try. If something doesn't work, learn from it and try again. Don't punish failure.

Summary

Recognition for changes is often overlooked. It's a critical element of sustainability. People need to understand something good happened because of their efforts. When they create a win for the organization, they need to know. Everyone else should be aware and thank them for their contributions.

Tell success stories. The more you do, the more the organization becomes aligned with and comfortable creating more wins. The ultimate Recognition is when someone outside of the organization tells the story of the changes the team made, as if they were part of the effort.

Recognition is the eighth and final spoke of The Wheel of Sustainability. Congratulations on getting this far. That's my Recognition for you.

The Wheel of Sustainability is strongest when all eight spokes are in place. It loses strength if a spoke is removed or is missing. Without the hub of Leadership Commitment, the Wheel falls apart. The next chapter is devoted to it. Read on. You've come too far to turn back now.

Recognition Takeaways:

How strong Leadership Commitment supports Recognition:

How weak Leadership Commitment damages Recognition:

What I can do to improve my approach to Recognition:

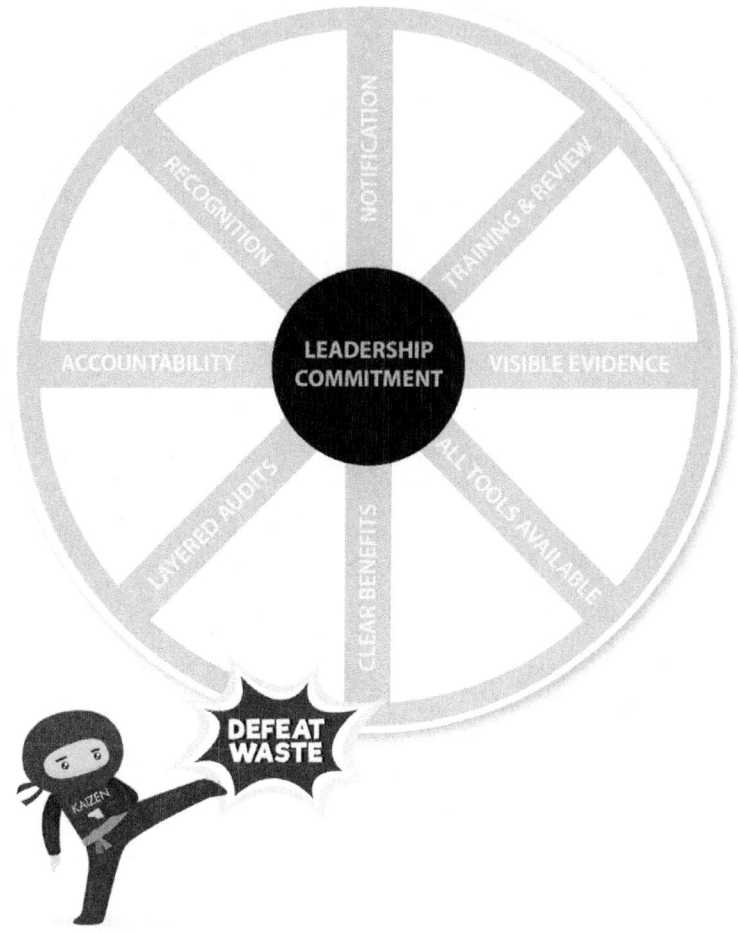

LEADERSHIP COMMITMENT

Leaders visibly commit to help, support, and provide everything necessary to give their teams a winning experience. They understand how changes impact performance, and promote all elements of the Wheel of Sustainability. They hold themselves accountable to sustain improved results.

Introduction

Prior chapters described the spokes of the Wheel of Sustainability in detail. You should now have an image of the Wheel and how it provides a foundation for lasting results. This chapter will examine how Leadership Commitment is applied to the Wheel to strengthen that foundation.

At the beginning of my continuous improvement journey, I'd take assignments, work with teams, and hope for the best. Sometimes the results didn't meet my expectations. It was due in part to some less than desirable behaviors:

- Team members "*floated*" into and out of the Kaizen event.
- Interruptions and distractions stopped progress.
- Team members weren't aware they were expected to spend the entire day in the Kaizen event.
- I once arrived at a factory to kick off a Kaizen event on Monday morning. None of the team members were there. They had to be called at home to come in for an afternoon kickoff. Needless to say, they weren't happy. Neither was I.
- Some members were resentful they weren't given a choice to participate. They said they were "*volun-told*".
- There was no charter for the event.
- The team leader complained he didn't want the responsibility.
- There was skepticism of support for the team's efforts at the end of the event. I am used to this at the beginning. It's troubling when it's at the end too.

Outcomes were hit or miss. I felt we could accomplish more. I worried the results would degrade after the team broke up or I went home. I knew we needed Leadership Commitment. I didn't know how to acquire it.

Over the years, I encouraged leadership to support team efforts. I didn't make much headway. I didn't understand why they didn't back the teams and their breakthrough solutions more strongly.

It was my fault.

I didn't provide an image of what strong Leadership Commitment looks like. I am now able to. It's the Wheel of Sustainability.

Principles of Leadership Commitment

- Everything is done to ensure a winning experience for the team.
- The answer to any team request is "*yes*".
- The work of the team is the most important thing going on at the time.
- Leaders devote time, energy, attention, and resources to benefit the work of the team.
- Preparation for the Kaizen event is just as important as the event itself.
- Once the Kaizen or project is over, the real work begins.

Success Stories

350 Employees Became 350 Business Owners

An engineered wood flooring plant in Kentucky was losing money. Yields were deteriorating. The plant needed help to reverse their losses and invited me for a site visit. After reviewing performance and discussing issues with the leadership team, we took a Gemba walk.

Safety was clearly the top priority. There was signage and effective placement of supporting tools and materials to keep everyone safe. All members of the staff demonstrated their commitment to safety through their behavior and actions during the Gemba walk.

Production was the next priority. There were *hour by hour* production boards, and many other measures of productivity posted around the lines and in the offices.

There was no evidence of quality or yield focus to be found. We searched everywhere. Nothing showed employees what to do to reduce defects or improve yields.

We chartered a three-day Kaizen event to shift the plant from a culture of production to quality and yield. Jack, the Plant Manager, was unsure how it could be done in such a short time, but approved the charter. We put together a team comprised of the plant leadership team and two corporate guests to provide outside perspective.

We discussed adding production operators to the team. I felt they'd provide an unfiltered view of the current plant culture and what was needed to support their daily efforts to improve yield and quality.

Jack wasn't comfortable inviting them for the full three days. He wanted the leadership team to be free to say anything and didn't want to expose the staff's dirty laundry.

We agreed to a compromise: We'd invite the production operators to participate for two hours and share their perspective as the *Voice of the Customer*. They were invited for 9:30 a.m. on the first day of the Kaizen.

Jack kicked off the Kaizen event with words of encouragement and empowerment. He was ready to "*blow up*" the existing culture and systems if that's what it took to improve quality and yield. Most of the team were skeptical this was possible. They wondered why they weren't in the plant running operations.

After an ice-breaker, we reviewed our charter, Lean principles, and the Wheel of Sustainability. Next, we discussed the current priorities and culture of the plant. All team members valued safety first and then production. They thought quality and yield were next. They were about to get a dose of reality.

Six operators and two supervisors entered the room. They took their seats amongst team members and waited uncomfortably for what was next. They never had interacted with the leadership team in this setting. It also seemed like they weren't told why they were invited.

Jack thanked them for joining us and explained the purpose of the Kaizen event and their role as our Customers. They weren't impressed. I introduced myself and explained that we wanted their honest feedback about how the plant was run. They didn't believe me. My goal was for them to open up and tell us what they really thought, using a series of open-ended questions:

- What's the message you currently receive about the importance of quality and yield? Safety? Productivity?
- Are plant priorities clear or confusing? How do you know what they are?
- How do you decide to prioritize productivity versus quality and yield versus safety when you are in the middle of a production run?

Our Customers gave short, terse answers. Team members asked follow-up questions to show they were listening. Nothing shared was revealing or of high value.

After twenty minutes of questions and minimal answers, I asked, "If you could change one thing about how the plant is run, what would it be?"

Sally, a production operator, blurted out, *"If these **SUMBICHES** cared enough to come to work every day, things would be better!"*

Blushing, she put her face in her hands. The room roared with laughter and clapped with approval. Jack put his arm around Sally and thanked her for being open and honest. He wanted to know more about what she meant.

Sally raised her head and shared more with the team. She spoke about the behaviors of the staff and how they sent mixed messages about what was important. Because of this, employees were uncomfortable raising issues. There was a lack of trust. They didn't feel like their opinions mattered.

Our other Customers opened up and shared their thoughts. They talked about the leadership approach and how production trumped everything, except safety. They were concerned with all of the scrap being generated. They were worried that the plant wouldn't survive much longer without better customer focus and overall results. They shared their feelings, concerns, and ideas. Leadership was listening. We were getting somewhere.

After an hour, we exhausted all topics and thanked our Customers for joining us. There was clapping, handshakes, high fives, and hugs on their way out. Our Customers felt like they had contributed to something important. They cared about the company, its customers, and the impact the plant had on their families and the community.

The team now knew there was important work to do. The next step was to create a vision statement, emphasizing what their Customers needed to do their job. It didn't take long:

"Three hundred fifty business owners with a yield-first mindset making every plank matter. Close is not good enough – stop until the customer will be delighted. Encourage everyone to take the time to make it right the first time."

The rest of the time was spent developing the strategy and tactics to support and achieve their vision. They were aligned and had strong

Leadership Commitment around strengthening the culture of quality and yield. Examples of changes included:

- Posting the Vision statement at the plant entrance.
- Crew meetings to reestablish plant priorities.
- Redesigning production boards to emphasize quality and yield and relocating them closer to the production lines.
- Scrap bins labeled with the value of the materials thrown away.

There was energy and excitement. By the end of the three days, you could see and feel the difference in the plant. Initial results were promising. Quality and yield improved to record levels. Beyond that, 350 employees acted like business owners and were aligned around what was most important to their customers, their families, and their community.

The Team Has More Power Than It Thinks

A leading consumer products company in Pennsylvania shipped millions of boxes of laundry detergent, deodorant, and other products to customers every week. Most of the time, large quantities of the same  products were shipped together. Distribution center employees picked full pallets out of racks, placed one label on each pallet, and loaded them onto a truck. In recent years, they entered into a supply agreement with Amazon. It turned their process upside down.

Amazon ships any quantity of products, from one box to a truckload of boxes to their customers. Their customers expect to receive their order rapidly and properly labeled. Amazon required a label on every box shipped to their distribution center, regardless if a pallet was full of the same items.

As an example, 150 boxes of deodorant fit on a full pallet. If these boxes were shipped to Target or Walmart, only one label was required on the pallet. If they were going to ship the same pallet of deodorant to Amazon's distribution center, they were required to put one label on every box. That's 150 labels.

Amazon required delivery to its distribution center in four days or less. This was much faster than the company had to deliver for any of their other customers. If deliveries were late, the company was fined by Amazon.

As the years went by, Amazon business increased dramatically. Distribution center staff were added to keep up, but they weren't able to meet the strict delivery requirements. The company accumulated $1.2 million annually in fines. At this point, they called me to help solve the problem.

Angela was the Distribution Center Manager. We took a Gemba walk to identify improvement opportunities. They were applying their large volume/low product diversity approach to the small volume/high product diversity of Amazon orders. We also learned they didn't receive Amazon orders in a timely or predictable fashion. This caused them to staff the distribution center in ways that made people wait for orders to pick and ship.

Based on our observations, we chartered a three-day Kaizen event to solve this problem:

Develop a system to safely meet the growing Amazon demand, while meeting delivery requirements. Reduce $1.2 million in annual late delivery fines to $600,000 or less.

We set these objectives:

- Reduce Amazon late delivery fines to less than $600,000 annually.
- Deliver 80 percent of all Amazon orders in 4 days or less.
- Increase Amazon order productivity by 25 percent or more.
- Implement 2 safety improvements per team member.

Angela demonstrated her Leadership Commitment by taking on the role of team leader. She picked team members who cared about solving the problem and had the will to win. She invited key employees from the distribution center and corporate team members to provide customer perspective and who had the authority to implement system changes.

Angela notified all team members that the event was critical to the continued success of the company. She set expectations for full participation for the three days. She made a compelling case and received full commitment from everyone she invited.

On the morning of the first day, Angela explained the problem from her point of view. She asked team members to keep an open mind and be willing to challenge traditional thinking. Next, the corporate Amazon Customer Service Manager presented the *"Voice of the Customer"*. You could feel the urgency and need for change and improvement. Next, we reviewed Lean principles and improvement techniques.

We took a Gemba walk to the Distribution Center office. Our first stop was at a computer workstation.

Me: "Can you explain what's happening here? Actually, what's not happening?"

Wendy (team member): "I'm waiting for Amazon orders to arrive from corporate."

Me: "What do you mean? Don't orders come in all the time?"

Wendy: "They do, but we don't see them until corporate transfers them to us. I can't give out assignments to pick Amazon orders until I receive them. We don't have any meaningful work to do while we wait."

Angela: "Why do you have to wait for corporate to issue Amazon orders? Aren't there any?"

Wendy: "Oh yes. The orders must have come in at corporate after 6 last night."

Angela: "Why does that matter?"

Wendy: "Corporate enters Amazon orders manually when they're received. By 6, everyone at corporate leaves for the day."

Angela: "What happens to those orders?"

Wendy: "They wait until someone comes in the next morning and enters them. It might be 10 or later before we see them. If orders come in Friday night, we won't see them until Monday morning."

Angela: "Our employees work around the clock, seven days a week. They aren't able to prepare Amazon orders between 6 p.m. and 10 a.m. most days. Sometimes they wait longer than that for meaningful work."

This was a big opportunity for improvement. More questions were asked. Team members were writing ideas on their Post-it notes.

We left the office and continued our Gemba walk. We observed physical and system issues negatively impacting safety and productivity. Many more ideas were written. After two hours, we returned to the meeting room and reviewed our observations and ideas.

Following the review, the team mapped the current process on a wall using Post-it notes. They made estimates of the time it took to complete each step.

Next, they identified *pain points* and *opportunities* and placed them on the process map. There were many. I directed them to identify the *opportunities* that would result in the greatest reduction in time and improvement in customer service. Simply put, work on the steps that took the longest time. Streamlining those steps would generate the maximum lead time reduction and customer service improvement. All work had to be within control of the team.

Some steps took more than 8 hours. Others took up to 24 hours or more in some cases. Those were our targets. The team reviewed all steps and voted to work on the highest impact opportunities, except for one.

They avoided the step called, *"Wait for orders from corporate"*. This step was identified to take anywhere from 90 minutes to more than 60 hours (if an order came in on a Friday evening). When improved, it would significantly impact overall results.

I challenged the team to focus on improvements to *"Wait for orders from corporate"*. They didn't feel they could make changes without proper approvals. Angela reminded them they were empowered by the fact they were the Kaizen team chosen to solve this critical business problem.

If they didn't feel they could unilaterally make changes, they should *"phone a friend"* for advice and approval. They wanted to automate Amazon order entry. Big box retailers (Walmart, Target, and others) already had automated order entry. Because this idea wasn't new, it should have been possible to implement quickly.

Ruth, a corporate team member, left the room to make a phone call to Jerry. He had the authority to approve the idea. After ten minutes, she returned.

Ruth: "I tried to reach Jerry, but he's out sick today. I'll try again tomorrow. Hopefully, he'll be in the office then."

Me: "We have three days to solve this problem. We don't have time to wait for Jerry to recover."

Ruth: "I know we don't have time. What do you suggest I do?"

Me: "Do you happen to have Jerry's home phone number?"

Ruth: "Seriously? Of course, I don't."

Me: "Are you willing to drive to Jerry's house, knock on his door, and ask for approval?"

Ruth: "You've got to be kidding! Jerry lives near corporate, which is two hours away from here. I'm not going to go to his house and bother him while he's sick."

Me (I wasn't kidding): "Okay, that might be an extreme request. Is there another way you can think of to get the approval we need?"

Ruth: "Well, now that you mention it, I could call Jerry's manager and see what she thinks."

Jerry's manager was in an all-day meeting and wasn't available either. Ruth knew what I was going to ask next. She called the group Vice President. She explained the situation and the approval she was seeking. She was told that Alice, another team member, had the authority to approve the request. Ruth came back into the room, met with Alice, and secured approval.

A corporate team member with programming skills had been listening to the conversation. She was working on the program while approval was being secured. Ten minutes later, Amazon order entry was automated. The team was so motivated by their win, they implemented many other improvements. Letting nothing stand in their way, the team beat all of the Kaizen objectives.

At the report out, they described how the only thing getting in the way of improvement was their way of thinking. Once they realized they were empowered, they couldn't lose. As of this writing, late delivery fines from Amazon have remained at zero.

The next story illustrates how Leadership Commitment can be found anywhere in the world.

From Russia with Love

I was asked to help our Russian ceiling tile manufacturing plant execute their annual Value Stream Mapping Kaizen (VSM). I had traveled to Russia two years earlier, during construction of the plant (Chapter 5 – *Saving Is Not Saving*). I worked with the operations team and helped them improve material flow over a two-week period as they prepared for the opening of the plant. This time, my responsibility was to coach their Lean Leader and help him organize and facilitate the VSM.

I met Ivan on Sunday afternoon at the plant. My goal was to prepare him and give him some tips on engaging the workforce and getting quick results during the Kaizen. He was familiar with Lean principles and facilitation techniques.

He was frustrated by the culture of the leadership team and didn't expect much engagement during the VSM. I assured him we'd get strong engagement and quick results. I wasn't aware of the cultural challenges ahead.

In Russia, if someone at a higher level in the organization is speaking, lower levels don't generally speak or voice differing opinions. Things took longer to accomplish. There was also a language barrier to deal with.

We agreed to use a modified Value Stream Mapping approach. Rather than diving into great detail when mapping the process, we'd stay at a high level. The team would map the *current state* and then identify opportunities for improvement.

On the first day, I was in a meeting room with thirty team members and seven interpreters. Each interpreter was paired with an English-speaking participant. When a Russian team member said something, the interpreter spoke into a microphone and English was relayed to our headsets. When English-speaking team members spoke, the interpreters translated their words into Russian.

Amazingly, there was only a two-second delay from the time someone spoke in Russian, to the time I heard the English in my ear. It was hard to concentrate at first, but it didn't take long to find a comfortable rhythm for the facilitation.

After introductions and a review of the Voice of the Customer, we took a Gemba walk. Team members were instructed to take yellow Post-it notes and Sharpies with them. They wrote observations and ideas in real time instead of trying to remember them. It would form the basis of the improvement efforts we'd identify later in the session.

Returning to the meeting room, we mapped the *current state* process on a wall. All team members were encouraged to write process steps and waiting steps on yellow Post-it notes and then place them where they thought they should go. Most wrote in Russian. If something was written incorrectly, I never knew.

If an error or better way to write a step was identified, team members were to replace or rearrange the step on the map. When we exhausted all steps, the team reviewed the map and made sure they had the correct steps and sequence.

If someone didn't immediately engage, I encouraged them to verify things were accurate from their perspective. Everyone participated, regardless of position.

Next, team members were directed to look at the steps and put a mark on the ones they felt caused the most problems or *pain* in the process. Once we saw the steps with the most marks, the team was challenged to brainstorm ideas to solve the biggest problems, writing ideas on blue Post-it notes.

After all ideas were written, it was time to review them. I showed Ivan how to give everyone *equal voice*. This was accomplished by going around the room, one person at a time, one idea at a time. The idea on the Post-it was spoken out loud and placed on flip chart paper for everyone to see. Then, the next person shared one of their ideas. We continued until we exhausted all ideas in the room.

Team members were then directed to review all ideas and place a mark on their five favorites. The ideas with the most marks were the highest priority ideas for the team to pursue. We were able to quickly reduce 240 ideas down to the top 25.

The group was divided into four-member sub-teams. They were directed to pick one of the top twenty-five ideas and build it out into future work for the plant. There were eight sub-teams. By the end of the event, they would each need to work on three prioritized ideas.

After an hour and a half, everyone reported on their progress, one sub-team at a time. The rest of the team listened and provided feedback. One sub-team that had an idea worth $800,000 annually made no progress and didn't share anything with the rest of the team. After all sub-teams reported on their progress, I asked Ivan to join me with the sub-team that made no progress.

Me: "I really like your idea. It's worth a lot of money. Why haven't you made any progress? Do you need help?"

Elena (sub-team member): "We like our idea too, but we don't know what to do next."

Me: "Help me understand why you feel that way. What's holding you back?"

Elena: "Upper management won't approve our idea."

Me: "Why do you say that? Don't you think they'll support your idea?"

Alexi (another sub-team member): "It would save the company many rubles. It's just that no one with approval authority is with us. They won't understand our idea or support it."

Me: "Can we call someone with approval authority and explain the idea to them?"

Ivan: "This would be highly unusual. Maybe the team can work on something else."

Me: "No, no, no. This idea's too important to give up on. Give me a few minutes and let me see what I can do."

I stopped by the Plant Manager's office and reviewed the situation. He told me a high-level executive with approval authority was at the plant, but not available. She was working on another project. I asked him if he thought we could schedule a review with her. He gave me one of those looks I get from my wife when I do something she doesn't approve of. I decided to take action anyway. What were they going to do, deport me?

I grabbed Ivan and the sub-team. It was time to demonstrate Leadership Commitment and the *Spirit of Kaizen*. We were on a mission to get feedback. We walked over to the office the visiting executive was using and waited outside the door. She was on the phone. They tried to walk away, but I wouldn't let them.

The executive looked up from her call and noticed us. Instead of waving us in, she looked back down and continued her call. Ivan wanted to leave. "Not yet," I said. She looked up again, saw us still standing there, hesitated, and then motioned for us to come into the office. This was our opportunity.

As facilitator, I felt it would be easier for me to explain the situation. Luckily, she spoke English.

Me: "Sorry for the interruption. My name's Adam and I'm facilitating the VSM."

Natalia (the executive): "I'm Natalia. What's so urgent that you were standing outside my office impatiently?"

Me: "Sorry for that. Thank you for letting us interrupt your work. This team has an idea to save the company many rubles. Do you mind spending a few minutes with them? They need your input and approval."

Natalia: "Maybe later or tomorrow. I'm really busy right now."

Me (with sad puppy dog eyes): "Oh?"

Natalia: "Well, I have a few minutes until my next meeting. Then I need to get back to my work."

Me: "Thank you. I'm going to let Elena explain the idea."

Elena explained in Russian. I have no idea what she said. Natalia seemed interested. Many things were said between her and the other team members in Russian. Ivan whispered that Natalia offered advice on how to improve the idea. Fifteen minutes later, she told the team they had her full support and they should pursue their fantastic idea. We thanked her for her time. I told Natalia she had the *Spirit of Kaizen* and the Leadership Commitment to help us win. We left her to go back to her work.

Later, Natalia visited with the sub-team to see how they were progressing. Their enthusiasm spilled over to other team members. Before long, many additional ideas were developed to make the plant safer and more productive.

By the end of the VSM, the plant had a strategic road map designed to help it meet its goals for the next three years. Team members remarked they had never been in a session where everyone was given equal voice and so much was accomplished in a short amount of time. It turns out the only thing in their way was their thinking. No matter your cultural background, the *Spirit of Kaizen* can live in you.

The next story illustrates how leaders may have to change their behavior on the fly, to demonstrate their commitment.

Go to Gemba, even if You Don't Want to

I was hired to facilitate the second annual Value Stream Mapping (VSM) event for a leading consumer brands manufacturer in Pennsylvania. Facilitating their first VSM was my first paying job as a consultant. Our objective was to build on the prior year's results and strengthen their continuous improvement culture.

Mike, the Plant Manager, rarely shared direct feedback with me. I'm a storyteller and tend to ramble (shocking, I know). He's focused and gets right to the point. The Technical Manager, Allan, had worked with me at my prior company. I received Mike's feedback through him.

Our challenge was to increase the engagement of the floor associates and drive the team to Gemba more than in the first VSM. Partnering with Allan, we identified team members and activities to accomplish both objectives.

Mike set the expectation to *"Go to Gemba"* in his opening remarks on the first day of the VSM. Team members at all levels were actively engaged during the Gemba walk. Whenever an issue was raised, we went to see, rather than discuss it.

On the second day, the team mapped their *current state* Value Stream, identified pain points, and brainstormed improvements. Next, they prioritized the work to drive performance to higher levels in the coming years.

The group was divided into six sub-teams and directed to develop concept sheets for the highest value improvement ideas. Mike joined two production technicians and one engineer and worked on an idea to resolve a critical cat litter line performance problem.

Sitting at a table, they spent ten minutes reviewing the problem they were trying to solve. Then, they got paper and scissors and cut various shapes out of the paper. I watched them for a while, then rotated through other groups to make sure they were progressing on their assignments.

After completing one rotation, I returned to observe Mike's sub-team. He and the engineer were moving papers around to simulate the cat litter line. The two operators weren't participating and didn't look happy.

Me: "Sorry to interrupt your progress. What are you *all* working on?"

Mike: "We're trying to understand the current layout of the cat litter line so we can come up with alternatives to improve the situation."

Me: "What are you learning about the problem?"

Mike: "We're a little unsure of the location of some of the equipment and the location of the columns. We assume they're located right here (pointing to a large rectangular piece of paper on the table).

Me: "Hard to imagine it on a table. Have you considered going to Gemba first?

Mike: "What do you mean?"

Me: "How do you know there isn't something you're not considering from your vantage point in the meeting room?"

It looked like Mike wanted to say something that wouldn't have been very nice. Instead, he stood up and took his team out to the factory.

Five minutes later, Allan approached me with a wry smile.

Allan: "You sure got Mike's attention. He walked me to his office and said, 'that *darn* Adam kicked me out of the meeting room and made me go to Gemba!'"

Me: "I guess I did. Am I fired?"

Allan: "Of course not. I'm glad you did it. He needs to set the example by going to Gemba. It's the same behavior he was encouraging in the rest of the team."

Me (with a sigh of relief): "He took it well. I could see he was holding his feelings back and did the right thing. I hope they learn something important while they're out in Gemba."

When Mike's team returned, all four members were engaged and working with newfound energy. They identified something they had overlooked. It was helping them develop a better solution.

Mike admitted he should have gone to Gemba first before trying to solve the problem in the meeting room. I was glad to hear it. I told him I thought he was going to fire me. We both laughed.

Throughout the rest of the event "*Go to Gemba*" was the rallying cry for all team members. By the end, the plant had a continuous improvement strategy with breakthrough improvements in safety, productivity, customer service, and the Leadership Commitment to strengthen plant culture.

Less than Success Story

Macon Progress

Early in my career, I traveled to Macon, Georgia to help a team improve the reliability and safety of their ceiling tile fabrication line. In those days, hourly employees were rarely involved in improvement projects. My prior visits to the plant revealed that many of them were creative and cared deeply about the safety and productivity of the plant. They just needed to be given the opportunity to participate.

Carl, the Business Unit Manager, approved a fabrication line Rapid Improvement event (we didn't call them Kaizen events in those days) and selected team members. We had six production and maintenance associates and two supervisors. We started our work on Monday morning.

Even though this was a new experience, team members were enthusiastic and gave their all. We started making improvements almost immediately.

Something was missing. Carl didn't join the team at kickoff or any time during the day to see what we were doing. Although team members didn't seem to mind, it bothered me. We were solving critical performance problems, after all. I wondered why he wasn't interested in our progress. If you knew me, and I guess by now you do, you'd expect me to do something about it. And, it wouldn't be subtle.

After team members went home, I walked to Carl's office. I hoped to convince him to visit with us on Tuesday while we were doing our work. It would reinforce his support to the team and show him what his people were capable of accomplishing.

He was working on his computer. Once he acknowledged me, I shared my observations. I told Carl team members were working well together and were open to new thinking. He was glad to hear it. I then asked if he'd make time on Tuesday to join us and let the team show off their accomplishments. He told me he'd be tied up in meetings all day. If there was time, he'd stop by. I left his office frustrated. He made no commitment. Would he stop by during a break?

Improvements came faster on Tuesday. Team pride grew and we were having fun. Hourly employees stopped by to see what we were doing. Our work was being noticed and appreciated. After a long day, we hadn't been visited by Carl or any member of the management team.

I was determined to generate interest and leadership support. I returned to Carl's office and was told he left the plant early to play golf, watch a high school baseball game, or something else of higher priority. I was angry and probably should have left it alone, but I couldn't.

At a break on Wednesday, I walked back to Carl's office. Luckily (or unluckily), he met with me.

Me: "The team is doing great work and giving it their all. They've made many improvements. I'm really proud of them."

Carl: "That's great to hear."

Me: "Some crew members and maintenance technicians stopped by to see what we're doing. The team brightened up every time that happened."

Carl: "Is there a point to all this?"

Me: "Look, it's great that you're sponsoring our work. It's disappointing that no one from management has come out to the line at any time to see us."

Carl: "Okay, now hold on a minute. What are you *really* trying to say?"

Me: "I know how busy things are at the plant. For the sake of the team, it'd be great if you'd visit and demonstrate your *commitment* to them." I struck a nerve.

Carl: "Adam, if you're questioning my commitment, **you can do it from corporate headquarters!**"

All I could do next was dig myself out of a deep hole. I don't remember what I said. I wasn't fired and I wasn't sent home. That's a win. When I returned to the team, I tried not to let my disappointment show. We continued our work and significantly improved line performance.

On Friday, Carl and other management team members joined us for a tour of the line. Would he have shown up without our conversation? Was he forced to give me a team to work on one of his lines? Did the corporate office dictate my efforts? Was it something the plant actually requested? I'll never know. It doesn't matter. I learned a valuable lesson.

It was *my responsibility* to create a process to align with leadership and gain their commitment to the work of the team. It took me many years. Now, I have the Wheel of Sustainability. You do too.

Leadership Commitment at Home or in the Office

Peggy's Tool Box

I'm always organizing things around the house. One winter, I cut the shapes of my tools into foam and lined the drawers of my tool box. It looked so nice, I showed it to my family so they could admire it too. They humored me, but didn't seem very impressed.

On a trip to Costco, I bought a labeler. It seemed like something that might come in handy for one of my home organization projects. Peggy asked me what I needed with one. I wasn't sure, but it was inexpensive. What was the harm in having one?

Eventually, I went through all of the tubs stored in our basement and consolidated and disposed of things. From time to time, I got Peggy's permission to donate or throw things away. After each tub was completed, I put a label on it to identify contents and the date it was reviewed. That way, I wouldn't feel the need to do it again for a few years. I showed off my work. Once again, I was met with a less than excited reaction.

I took some grief for being so organized, but Peggy and I laughed about it often. She was also quietly organizing the kitchen. We'd go to a store and come back with plastic containers of various sizes.

One morning, while taking out my breakfast cereal, I noticed labels on the plastic containers in the pantry. All of a sudden, the labeler had purpose. The idea of organizing and making things visible, was beneficial to Peggy. More than that, she was committed to the idea.

I help out in the kitchen after dinner. Peggy washes the dishes and I dry them and put them away. I always forget which Pyrex goes where and have to be reminded often. One day, I asked why the Pyrex goes where it does and wouldn't it be better to store it differently? I was met with this explanation:

"Don't mess with my tool box and I won't mess with yours."

From then on, I haven't questioned Peggy's system. I get well fed and meals always come out on time, regardless of the number of ingredients or side dishes. I don't question the need for another container, pot, pan, or utensil. I reap the rewards.

Peggy's fully committed to her system. She sees the value of organization and ensures everyone knows and follows the standard. We receive Clear Benefits through the use of her tool box.

How to Develop Effective Leadership Commitment

The Wheel of Sustainability is my image of Leadership Commitment. In initial meetings with sponsor(s), I describe how teams will be engaged and empowered, how the Wheel will be used, how they can support the effort, and what's expected of them. Then, I look them in the eye to see how they react.

I watch for warning signs of weak Leadership Commitment. These are some examples:

- The Sponsor challenges the time required to execute the Kaizen event. They think it could be done in less time. I understand that it's preferable to use less time and resources. Using logic and experience, I determine the time required to ensure a win.
- Something *more important* is going on at the same time.
- There's little interest in engaging or empowering the workforce.
- There's low engagement or empowerment in the staff or workforce.
- The Sponsor or Leader thinks they're a Lean *"expert."*
- The Sponsor is not able or willing to kick off or join the team at any time during the Kaizen event.
- Team members aren't personally asked to participate by the Sponsor or Team Leader. Responsibility is delegated to others.
- Team members aren't expected to be *"all in"* during the Kaizen event.
- The Team Leader was assigned, and isn't aligned with the effort.
- The Sponsor wants the team to implement previously identified solutions.

- There hasn't been organizational communication in advance of the Kaizen event.
- There's little time allocated to prepare for the event.

Any one is no reason to walk away. If there are a few of these or others, it's time to reconsider the partnership. I won't deviate from my mission:

Provide a winning team experience.

Assessing Leadership Commitment

To accomplish my mission, I use a *site assessment* to assess Leadership Commitment. It takes approximately six hours and follows this process:

1. Meet the leadership team at their location. Observe their interactions and engagement.
2. Review the problem(s) they want to solve.
3. Take a Gemba walk to see the problem(s) in action and engage with those who deal with the problems. Observe leadership team engagement during the walk.
4. Review findings at lunch.
5. Create a path forward.
6. Build a charter for potential Kaizen events.
7. Review the Wheel of Sustainability and Leadership Commitment during a Kaizen event.
8. Review expectations once the Kaizen event is complete.
9. Review the day and gather feedback.

Here's how I use each element to assess and strengthen Leadership Commitment:

1. Meet the leadership team at their location

I arrive early to see how the leadership team starts their day. What's their energy level, urgency, and focus? We meet in a conference room, at a morning meeting, or some other activity that brings them together. It might be the *site assessment* that brings them together.

We get to know each other through initial introductions. Who's been invited to participate? What's their role? Are they interested in my visit? I discuss my process and map out the day. I watch their reactions to a six-hour commitment. Everyone isn't expected to participate the entire time. Not quite a job interview, I think of it more like a test drive.

2. Review the problems they want to solve

The leadership team describes problems they are most interested in solving. Using probing questions, I seek a deeper understanding and a sense of urgency. What are the reasons they feel the need for outside help? Are they speaking freely or holding back because the boss is in the room?

Observing the engagement, I want to see if they work as a team and if they're willing to empower others to solve critical problems.

3. Go see the problems in Gemba

We go to Gemba and look for evidence of the problems we discussed. Many think they're giving me a facility tour. They're certainly welcome to. My focus is on the areas and people impacted by the problems we reviewed.

Talking with people engaged in the process, I get their view of the problems. I introduce myself and then ask what they're doing and if they have any problems doing their job.

Sometimes they aren't comfortable speaking about problems with a visitor and a group of managers. Some think I'm an *auditor*. We know what people think of them (see Chapter 7).

Having had conversations earlier about problems in the area, I probe for evidence of them and ask questions related to the problems and my observations.

When people realize I'm aware of the problems, they tend to open up. I try to put them at ease and listen to their views. I write notes of who they are and what they tell me, verbatim. It's Visible Evidence that I'm listening to them. It helps me remember who said what and when.

Once the conversation is flowing, I watch to see how leadership engages. It's a positive sign if they're comfortable having their *dirty laundry* aired and participate in the conversation.

I seek many perspectives during the Gemba walk. Some will be having a good day, others won't. I want to know what it's like to work at the company and engage with the leadership team.

Six to twelve interactions will give me the information I need. Remember, I am not trying to solve the problems. I'm trying to understand what they are, how they affect people, and if I believe the leadership team will empower and engage their employees to win. The Gemba walk takes around two hours. Now it's time for lunch.

4. Review findings at lunch

There's a strategy around having lunch with the leadership team. How do they relate to each other in a more relaxed setting? Are they interested in my observations? What did they learn during the Gemba walk?

While we're eating, we're still working, and reviewing observations and findings. They tend to open up more about their situation. It's possible we may have uncovered hidden or unknown problems. I need to find out if they're interested in rescoping the work. They may want to know what I think and what to do next.

5. Develop a path forward

I've never visited a business that didn't have opportunities to make things better for their customers and their people. Now it's my opportunity to share my observations and suggestions. This is the next test of the leadership team's interest and commitment to improving.

I propose tactical and strategic improvements for their consideration. I provide examples of winning team experiences. Sometimes they're skeptical their teams will be able to achieve breakthrough results in a short time. If they don't have experience with Kaizen or other rapid improvement methods, they may not know what to expect.

One potential client said he thought it wasn't possible to make significant, sustainable improvements in a week or less. I didn't take it personally. He hadn't experienced *true* Kaizen. At least not the type of

Kaizen event I've facilitated. He'll either have to take a *leap of faith*, or decide not to take a chance on my approach.

It's now up to the leadership team. What do they want to do next? Most of the time, we're able to identify and schedule the first Kaizen event. Subsequent events rely on the success of the first one. That's a reasonable approach. I'd want to see results before I commit to additional work. Leaders don't yet have an idea of the level of resources, effort, commitment, and cost required at this point. They will soon. The next step is chartering.

6. Build the charter

The charter is a contract between the Sponsor and the team to solve a critical business problem.

Read the graphic linearly, from left to right. Don't move to the next element until you complete the preceding one. Rewrite and revise the charter as needed. Focus on one element at a time. The first step is to build a problem statement.

A. *Problem statement*

The problem statement should be clear, concise, challenging, and compelling. It's written from the point of view of the customer, the people who do the work, and/or the greater organization. It should contain measures of business impact. Examples include:

- Days it takes from customer order to delivery.
- Time it takes to answer a customer inquiry.
- Waiting time in an emergency room.
- The cost of downtime.
- The number of injuries.
- Number of traffic accidents resulting in fatalities.

The scope of the effort must be defined. We can't solve all problems in the company. It's good practice to narrow down to a point where the team is working on something in their control.

It's not unusual for a problem statement to start out vague and look like this example:

Our customers aren't happy with the service levels we provide. We must improve our service to the customer in order to stay profitable.

This statement doesn't tell us much. We can always improve on customer service. But what's the impact of poor service? After many hundreds of charters, I have been able to help transform the prior statement to something that looks like this:

Our average time from customer order to delivery is 8.5 days. This compares unfavorably to the industry average of 6.2 days. Each day above the average results in a loss of $800,000 in annual sales. In total, we are losing $1.8 million of annual sales opportunity. We believe this situation is mainly due to inefficiencies in the distribution center.

The purpose of this session is to reduce customer order to delivery time to 5 days or less, resulting in a total gain of $2.8 million of annual sales opportunity. The scope of this event will be the distribution center processes. There can be no adverse impact on safety or other business measures.

This statement is compelling, challenging, and clear. It's challenging to reduce time by 3.5 days, but it has enough value to commit a team to it. They will focus on the distribution center. If they uncover opportunities elsewhere, they'll save them for others to work on.

B. Objectives

When the problem is solved, what does it look like? What are the clear indications it has been solved? How do we define a *win*? Leadership must identify what they expect. Clear objectives do that.

In the example problem statement, one of the objectives might be: "Average order to delivery time of 5 days by the end of the year". It shouldn't be the only one. Consider holding other things constant or improving safety, quality, and/or cost. Don't sacrifice one business measure for another. I recommend adding at least one safety objective.

Based on the example problem statement, these are the objectives:

1. *Average order to delivery time of 5 days by December 31 of the current year.*
2. *One safety improvement implemented per team member.*
3. *No adverse impact on safety, quality, cost, or customer experience.*
4. *Standard work for all changes.*
5. *Implement the Wheel of Sustainability.*

The Wheel of Sustainability *must* be one of the objectives. It guarantees the team will sustain solutions implemented during the Kaizen event. It also reinforces Leadership Commitment.

C. The winning team

Who can help solve the problem? Once we understand the problem, scope, and objectives, we should choose team members who are interested, have process knowledge, feel the pain, and care. They may be the most vocal, passionate, grumpy, or frustrated people you know.

Assemble the strongest team with available resources. Most people want to win. Let's give them the opportunity. A successful Kaizen team includes:

- Three or more involved in the process where the *pain* exists – from different areas, shifts, or locations. Identify those who will challenge each other and represent the interests of others who aren't on the team. Why three? To break a tie. If there are more than three locations, areas, or shifts, use that number.
- One or more internal or external customers of the process.
- At least one internal or external supplier to the process.
- One manager or supervisor of the process. This person knows the broader picture and can acquire resources for the team as needed.
- One outside set of eyes. Someone who isn't directly connected with the process or from another location that isn't experiencing the same problem. This person shouldn't be the facilitator.
- Team Leader. Responsible for the successful implementation of team efforts. May be someone from the members listed above.
- Subject matter experts or other interested individuals.

- Facilitator – guides the team and is not part of the team. The Facilitator is not the Team Leader. The Facilitator is responsible for the process. The Team Leader is responsible for the content and the decisions of the team.

The size of the team is determined by the scope and complexity of the problem. There should be seven team members, at minimum. The team can grow significantly if you're not careful. I have facilitated teams of three and we were able to get a lot done, but it's challenging. Add a co-facilitator when the team has sixteen or more members. Committed leaders put the best possible team together.

Team members work together uninterrupted to solve the problem during the Kaizen event. They implement their solution. The charter is the contract with the team to solve a critical business problem. Leadership and the team honor the contract. Leaders support the solution and managing systems implemented by the team. Before the event, leaders don't know what the solution is. If they did, there wouldn't be a problem to solve or a need for the team.

As they work, the team will require help, resources, approvals, and anything else they come up with to solve the problem and sustain the solution. All elements of the Wheel of Sustainability will be implemented. Leadership must be committed and accountable to support all requests and elements. The answer must be *yes*, regardless of the request. This is Leadership Commitment. Sometimes, it requires a *leap of faith*.

If you're *unwilling* to make this level of commitment, cancel the Kaizen event. If you go forward with this attitude, you'll frustrate the team and waste their time. If you *are* willing to provide this level of Leadership Commitment and support, you're going to *win*.

D. Owner of the output = Team Leader

The Team Leader owns the output. They have to live with the results. They have a vested interest. They'll make sure the team does the right thing. If the team is struggling to make a final decision, they're the tiebreaker. In my early experiences, I didn't always have a Team Leader who was owner of the output. This was a mistake and results suffered because of it.

Chartering is a process. It's not unusual to need many iterations before finalizing the charter. I have found many people who have difficulty writing charters. Because of this, I write the first draft and then let the leadership team edit my work. It's vitally important they align around the charter and can explain it to potential team members and their sponsor(s).

7. Review the Wheel of Sustainability

The leadership team needs to understand the Wheel of Sustainability. They must have an idea of the systems to be implemented and their role in support of those systems. I review the Wheel in detail and assess Leadership Commitment through their interest and engagement.

I highlight the effort required to support implementation of the Wheel. If leaders think it's too much effort, we shouldn't proceed. If they have no prior experience with sustainment, they won't know how vital it is until they see it in action. They are now aware of what it requires and of expectations of their Leadership Commitment.

8. What happens when the Kaizen event is over?

Most people think the Kaizen event is the hard part and once it's over, they can go back to their normal lives. Nothing is further from the truth. It's now time to do everything to implement, support, and hold Accountability to the solutions and systems created by the team.

More time and effort will be spent reinforcing the changes than most people expect. The leadership team must be prepared and willing to put in the work.

Knowing I won't be in the facility the day after the Kaizen (most of the time), I represent expectations in a way the leadership team can support. This is another test of their Leadership Commitment. If they agree to do what's necessary, we can proceed. One more step remains.

9. Review the day and gather feedback

I've tried to represent everything necessary to ensure a winning Kaizen experience and what it takes to sustain results. I've demonstrated my approach. It's time for feedback. It's a quick test to see if we're aligned, they believe breakthroughs are possible, they want to work with me, and they have the Leadership Commitment required to succeed.

I ask three questions:

1. What did you like *most* about my visit and approach?
2. What did you like *least* about my visit and approach?
3. What could I do better on a future visit to a potential client?

I write their feedback on a flip chart. It's hard not to be defensive or explain my methods during the review. It's their perception of my approach and it indicates how well we may be able to work together. It can be challenging to hear the truth. It tells me if we're aligned and have the best chance to win. I take the flip chart with me and reflect on the feedback once I get home.

The site assessment tells me if there is the Leadership Commitment required to move forward and assure a winning experience for the organization.

After the Kaizen event is over

Earlier I said that the Kaizen event may feel like the most difficult work. The moment the event is over is when the real work begins. The team has just solved a critical business problem. They've identified and implemented solutions no one else was able to before they came together. They've installed all elements of the Wheel of Sustainability and created plans to deploy their solution.

This is where Leadership Commitment gets its ultimate test. Leadership must support all elements of the Wheel as designed, even if they don't fully agree with the team's solution.

Leaders participate in Notification, Training and Review, and demonstrate the use of Visible Evidence and All Tools Available. They reinforce Clear Benefits, conduct Layered Audits, hold themselves Accountable, and Recognize the effort through stories that drive the culture of change.

They give team members time and support to fully implement the solution. They must be willing to adjust their behavior as they learn about the changes on Gemba. If they uncover new issues, they must work with members of the Kaizen team to learn about and resolve them.

Leaders can't return to their prior behaviors. It's easy to fall back to old habits. They must resist temptation and honor their commitment. It all sounds good in theory. It's hard in practice. The team has used the Wheel of Sustainability to develop solutions that benefit the organization. They may have missed something. The Wheel uncovers most, but not all, critical issues to be resolved.

Sometimes the Kaizen team must reconvene to work on new issues. Or, another team may be assigned. Regardless, it's a test of Leadership Commitment. Allow the time to reconvene or put a new team together. Don't give up. Keep learning and keep trying. Commit to the Wheel of Sustainability and help your teams sustain their win.

Mistakes to Avoid

Not applying the Wheel of Sustainability

If you're unwilling to use the Wheel of Sustainability, you indicate the work isn't important enough to sustain. Teams are going to work hard to make improvements. If you're unwilling to support and implement the Wheel, you'll frustrate your teams and will see recurrence of the problems.

Not providing necessary time or resources

If the team asks for three days to accomplish their charter, don't ask why they can't do it in two. Challenging their request may feel disrespectful. Don't assign random team members. Resource and support the winning team.

Being unavailable

The team may need your help to resolve a critical issue. If you're unable to make yourself available, they may not get the information, perspective, support, or encouragement they need.

Being invisible

The team needs Leadership to be visible in the process. If you're unwilling to spend time in the process, demonstrating your understanding and commitment, the organization won't value the changes and will go back to the old way of doing things.

Lacking understanding of the changes

People in the organization will seek out leaders to help them understand the value of the changes. If leaders don't understand, it sends a strong message of the lack of importance of the new standard.

Lacking alignment

The worst thing to say to someone who wants to understand why they must change is *"they're making us do this,"* or *"because I said so."* If leadership isn't aligned around the changes, the organization won't value them.

Summary

The Wheel of Sustainability is only as strong as the elements binding it together. As I stated earlier, the spokes connect the Wheel to the central hub of Leadership Commitment. Removing a spoke reduces the strength of the Wheel. Without Leadership Commitment, the Wheel falls apart.

The Wheel provides an image of what's expected from leaders as they support improvement efforts. When they truly understand what's required of them and make a conscious decision to utilize the Wheel of Sustainability, they give the organization the best opportunity to create lasting results.

The Wheel of Sustainability was developed with the premise that people care about the problems they're attempting to solve. Committed leaders willingly devote time, energy, attention, and resources to the effort. They engage and empower their teams to implement the Wheel of Sustainability and win.

Leadership Commitment Takeaways:

How strong Leadership Commitment supports sustainability:

How weak Leadership Commitment damages sustainability:

What I can do to improve my approach to Leadership Commitment:

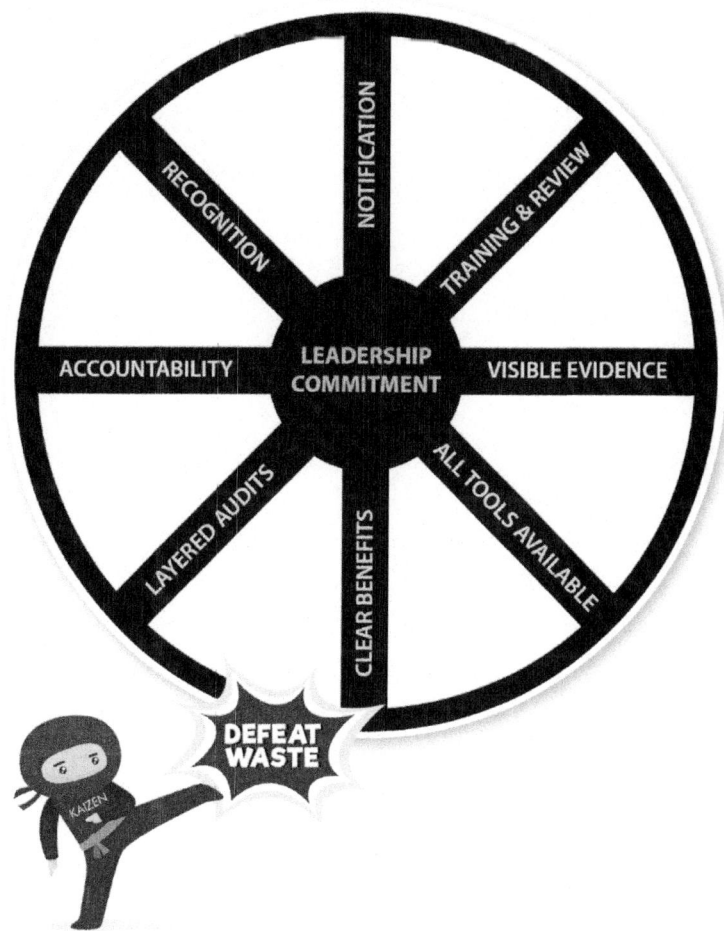

A LEADERSHIP COMMITMENT TOUR
AROUND THE WHEEL OF SUSTAINABILITY

A LEADERSHIP COMMITMENT TOUR AROUND THE WHEEL OF SUSTAINABILITY

Leadership Commitment is vital to the lasting results we seek. It is the hub that holds together the Wheel of Sustainability. To reinforce its importance, I offer the following guidance on how Leadership Commitment should be applied to the Wheel and each element to ensure lasting results.

The Wheel of Sustainability

Know the Wheel of Sustainability. Be firm in your convictions that every element is important and must be implemented. Be an advocate. Others may not understand the Wheel. Describe it and its importance to the organization.

- Post a picture of the Wheel of Sustainability in your office.
- Start conversations about it.
- Share stories of successful use of the Wheel.
- Hand out copies of this book to help the organization understand the reasoning behind the Wheel.
- Start a Wheel of Sustainability book club.

- Review one element at a time as part of your leadership team meeting agenda.

Notification

Provide Notification of changes to the organization. Participate as a Sponsor. You must know *what* the changes are, *why* they're important, and the expectations of those responsible to implement and follow them. Those you notify will watch you to assess your feelings. If you believe in the changes, the organization will follow your lead. You must believe it's unacceptable to deviate from the new standard. If you believe, they will too.

Training and Review

Allocate time for people to be trained using Tell, Show, and Do. Recognize the need for one-on-one engagement. Support the request for resources and be willing to allow extra time, if necessary. Ask for personal training from one of the team members. Treat Training and Review as an investment in future results. The payoff is huge.

Visible Evidence

Look for visuals that reinforce the new standard. Point them out and engage in conversations around them. Be aware and familiar with how they are used. What does red mean? What are you supposed to do? How are you supposed to engage and help? How do you *rally to the red*? Don't assign blame. Celebrate when Visible Evidence revealed deviations and drove the organization back to standard. Recognize when people are doing the right things.

All Tools Available

Approve the time, materials, and labor to provide the proper tools required in any and all locations as defined by the team. Don't set a budget. If the team buys more than necessary, they can return what's not needed. The team has determined the value of having what's needed without searching for or transporting things. Be firm in your convictions that people must have what they need where they need it to do their job in the safest, most productive manner possible. The answer to any reasonable request for tools is always "*yes*".

Clear Benefits

Talk with those following the standard. Understand their perspective. Are the changes helping them do their job in a way they believe is safer, more productive, and less stressful? If so, reinforce those benefits. If they don't see the Clear Benefits, review their feedback with the team or help them understand what they may be overlooking. Reinforce cause and effect. They may not be aware the tools they need are right where they need them and are continuing to carry them as they always have. Make the connection to the positive impact on critical performance measures. Tell stories and promote the wins.

Layered Audits

Participate and engage regularly in Layered Audits. Look for evidence of audits being conducted. Encourage others to participate. Conduct informal and formal audits. Rotate times, locations, and system aspects. Sign off to let everyone know you were there. Don't back off the schedule. If people stop auditing, demand they start back up with renewed commitment and focus. If a problem is found during the audit, take the time to resolve it or help those who can. If an executive or someone from another location is visiting, take them with you. Use their outside eyes to uncover issues others missed. Share the value of auditing with them, so they can take it back to their home location. Tell stories of issues uncovered and corrected because of the audit. Implement a Gemba walk and use it as an audit.

Accountability

Look for evidence people are following the standard. If they are, take the time to thank them. If they aren't, engage with them and help them follow the changes as defined. Don't delegate responsibility or try to remember to return later. Engage immediately. Reinforce the importance of the changes and your Leadership Commitment to them. If you're late to a meeting, explain yourself. Make sure others know how important it is to follow the standard. Nothing is more important. Your Leadership Commitment reinforces that belief.

Recognition

Identify and tell stories of positive results that came about because of the changes. Encourage others to do so as well. Look for cause and effect. Make measures of success visible. Add a discussion of success stories to the leadership team meeting agenda. Celebrate when milestones are achieved. Share success stories with the internal and external organization. Create opportunities to expand success to other areas. Promote the success to other locations. Get others interested. Look for the moment that someone who wasn't involved in the changes tells the story as if they were. This is a win.

Leadership Commitment

Know what it is and what it looks like. Be able to describe how leaders should engage with the Wheel of Sustainability. Look for evidence of strong and weak Leadership Commitment. You don't need a formal title to have Leadership Commitment. Identify those who act like leaders and recognize their behaviors and actions.

Learn the chartering process. Be firm in your convictions that Kaizen and project teams must be properly supported in order to create a winning experience.

The Wheel of Sustainability is a system. Implementing all elements gives it the strength to ensure critical results live on and aren't dependent on one person. Immediately after implementing changes, demonstrate Leadership Commitment. Don't back off. Don't reduce energy and effort. The work is too important. Leadership Commitment will help your team win.

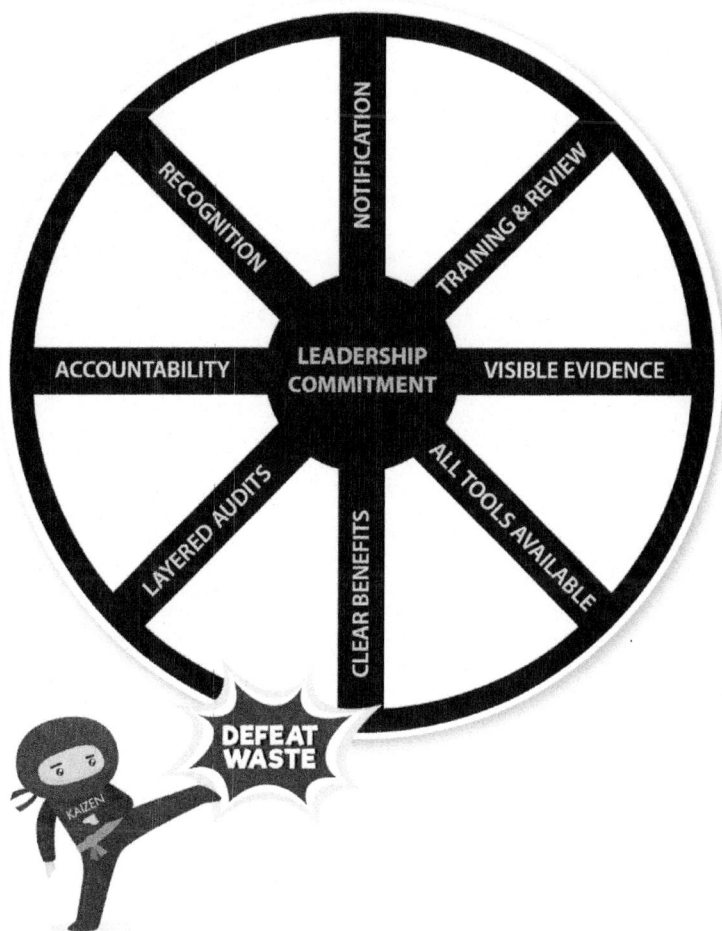

FINAL THOUGHTS

FINAL THOUGHTS

People are the key to improvement.

Some people think learning to use tools will help solve problems, change culture, and rise above the competition. I used to think this way. Tools are only part of the equation. They're meaningless if we don't have the desire to make things better and aren't willing to adapt.

The Wheel of Sustainability may appear to be another problem-solving tool. It was designed to be more than that. It's a *system* that ensures solutions live on. The Wheel identifies, elevates, and sustains results teams strive to achieve.

The Wheel of Sustainability uncovers possibilities. It causes teams to think of their efforts holistically. It drives them to involve and engage others. The Wheel leverages psychology and my observations of how people react to changes:

- Clear Benefits uses feedback and input to create buy-in and commitment.

- Training and Review reinforces how much we care for others by taking the time to Tell, Show, and Do in a one-on-one engagement. Trainer and learner create a common understanding and strengthen their relationship.
- Notification demonstrates belief in doing the right thing through the description of *why*, not *what*.
- Layered Audits drive us to engage and solidify understanding and importance of the changes.
- Accountability encourages personal responsibility to help people do the right thing.
- Visible Evidence supports a culture of help and teamwork. Status can be assessed and help can be provided by anyone at any time.
- All Tools Available strengthens commitment to provide everything necessary to accomplish work in the safest, most productive way possible. The answer to a request is always *"yes"*.
- Recognition shares stories we want everyone to know and feel good about. The stories end with a *win* for people and the organization.
- Leadership Commitment relies on the strength of our resolve to do the right thing at all times. We give of ourselves for the greater good.

The common theme is leaders demonstrate they care about their people by implementing a system to ensure beneficial results live on. That system is the Wheel of Sustainability.

It almost sounds like I knew what I wanted to do prior to building the Wheel. I assure you it's not the case. I learned by failing many times. I studied what worked and what didn't. I recognized the need to build a system and identified the elements necessary to sustain critical results.

In early iterations, there were fewer elements. I used what I had, and found results to be better than we had achieved in prior work. There were still issues with eroding results. Through study, I uncovered what was missing. I didn't discover the Wheel of Sustainability, it discovered me.

In 2014, I attended a conference in Ohio. I met continuous improvement practitioners from all over the world. We had many discussions of our efforts to help teams improve processes. At lunch, I sat at a table with a small group. They were talking about the difficulty of sustaining results at the end of Kaizen events. I told them I had developed a system for sustainment. They wanted to know more.

I drew eight circles surrounding a bubble in the middle:

I called it Adam's Sustainability Molecule (get it?). They were intrigued. Three of them drew it on what they had, including napkins. I knew I had created something of value. It was helping me and now it would help them.

The format of a Molecule didn't resonate. I needed a framework that was easier to visualize and explain. Eventually, it became the Wheel of Sustainability.

Give the Wheel a try the next time you're working on a problem you want to remain solved. Test your solution against all elements. If one isn't represented, consider how you might create and implement it. Try your solution, simulate it, and go to Gemba. Challenge yourself and your team. Most importantly, make sure you are committed and have the support of your leaders.

You might be under the impression the Wheel of Sustainability can only be used at the beginning of an improvement effort, project, or Kaizen event. Nothing could be further from the truth. It can be implemented at any point in the life of a change, project, or improvement effort. It's ideal before changes are developed, but it's possible and beneficial after changes are implemented. These are some tips to implement the Wheel at various stages in a project, improvement effort, or Kaizen event.

In the middle of an effort or project

You've spent time working on a project and are preparing to implement changes. You're concerned you haven't done enough to ensure your results will live on. Don't despair. Follow these steps:

1. Print out a graphic of the Wheel.
2. Meet with your Sponsor and provide an overview of the Wheel of Sustainability. Hand them the graphic. Explain how it will help the team improve their implementation plan.
3. Confirm Sponsor interest.
4. Take your Sponsor to Gemba. Look for examples of the elements of the Wheel. Ask your Sponsor to identify what they see. Look for Visible Evidence, All Tools Required, and/or Layered Audits. These are the easiest elements to identify visually. If they're not seen, they're not there.
5. Make your initial pitch to utilize the Wheel of Sustainability. Look for affirmation.
6. Assess the work against the Wheel and identify elements to be created or strengthened. You'll need Sponsor support, engagement, and some funding.

7. Look your Sponsor in the eye. If they agree and don't flinch, you're ready to take the next step. You have the necessary Leadership Commitment to proceed.

8. Meet with your team, review the Wheel of Sustainability, and take a deep dive into each element. The team must feel implementation of the Wheel will have Clear Benefits to them and the organization.

9. Facilitate your team to identify what's missing and how it might impact results. Go to Gemba to verify the elements to be developed or strengthened.

10. Identify the value of implementing or strengthening elements. How many mistakes could be avoided? How much would effort be reduced? How much safer, more productive, or responsive to the customer will the organization be? Strengthen their belief in the Clear Benefits.

11. Develop implementation plans for each element. Assign owners and get to work.

12. Test your plans, get feedback, and improve from there.

13. Engage your Sponsor to demonstrate Leadership Commitment for implementing the Wheel. It will reinforce the importance to the team, to the Sponsor, and to you.

14. Build metrics for the effort. Design the implementation of the Wheel in a way that reinforces the positive results you're trying to achieve.

15. Use all elements of the Wheel to develop the sustainable approach to implement the Wheel of Sustainability. It will give you the opportunity to practice using the Wheel and improve the chances for a win.

16. Tell stories about the Wheel, be accountable to it, and expand awareness and Recognition of it.

17. Repeat steps as necessary.

If the Wheel wasn't implemented and results don't meet expectations or are deteriorating

If your team has implemented changes that aren't delivering and sustaining the results you expected, don't give up. Apply the Wheel to existing changes and make the necessary corrections to drive sustainability. It takes focus and determination.

If the results are important, you should be able to get your Sponsor to approve the time and resources for the additional work. This is a test of Leadership Commitment. View the existing changes using the lens of sustainability. Using anecdotal evidence, identify the missing elements of the Wheel. Some may be in place, but may need to be strengthened.

Most teams want to move on to the next thing. Don't move on to something else. Back up, assess the situation, and apply the Wheel as needed. It should be relatively simple to identify missing elements and imagine how to add them in a practical and sustainable way.

If you have difficulty, you have options: engage your Sponsor, team members, or call someone who is more familiar with the Wheel. Elements of the Wheel don't have to be perfect; they need to be considered and well thought out. Your attempt to implement a missing element makes things better. That's the idea behind continuous improvement:

A little better every day.

During a multiple day Kaizen event

My Kaizen teams implement the Wheel of Sustainability as part of the event. They don't wait until after it's over. The Wheel is introduced on the first day for awareness and expectation for its use. I hand out a graphic and review each element in detail. Team members don't yet know what to do with the information. The team begins to think about the Wheel and what it might mean in context with their work.

On Day two, I challenge the team to implement the Wheel in conjunction with their improvements. They must demonstrate each element. If they have difficulty, I coach them through it. For example, if they've never seen a Layered Audit, I provide examples. Or push them hard enough to storm out of the room and own their solution, like Sammy and the Weld shop team did in Chapter 7 (*Owning Their Solutions in the Weld Shop*).

How many hours does it take to build all elements of the Wheel of Sustainability in relation to the changes? Like any good question, the answer is: *it depends*. The more people utilize the Wheel in the development of the changes or improvements, the easier and faster it is to implement.

Teams who are using the Wheel as part of their solutions will spend between two and eight hours to implement it effectively. The more familiar they are with the Wheel, the easier it will be to implement. Is the extra time worth the effort? I certainly think so. Why else would I have written this book? The return on investment is a reduction in rework, lower likelihood of problem recurrence, simpler training requirements, and less follow-up.

Prior to the start of a project, Kaizen event, or other improvement effort

In Chapter 10, I described how I introduce the Wheel of Sustainability to my Sponsors and use it to test their Leadership Commitment. I recommend you use a similar approach. Start with your Sponsor. Test Leadership Commitment, go to Gemba, reinforce the concept of the Wheel. Charter the event. Build the team. Once you receive approval, introduce the Wheel to your team.

Hand a graphic of the Wheel to team members. Some will keep it, write notes on it, or put it up on the wall of their work space. Some teams that haven't worked with me personally were exposed to the Wheel by members of teams I facilitated. I heard they used the Wheel and reported to their Sponsors about their success because of it. I am pleased to know the value of the Wheel has spread beyond my personal experience with teams. This is the Recognition I seek.

When a team is considering a change or improvement effort, review the Wheel and identify how to use each element to strengthen the chance for success. If the team requires their Sponsor to engage with any of the elements, they must initiate the conversation as soon as possible. Is their Sponsor willing to conduct a weekly audit? How will they hold themselves accountable if they see someone not following the new standard?

If the team is making a focused effort to implement the Wheel, I challenge them to show how they will apply each element. What does it look like? How will it be demonstrated? What are the benefits of it? They have to report back to each other. This strengthens their understanding and commitment.

Team members are required to test elements on others who aren't part of the team. One of my favorite sayings is: "*There are twelve people on the team and hundreds of others on the team too; they just don't know it.*" The earlier the team tests their ideas with others and gathers feedback, the sooner they can make changes or improvements. They gain a broader view of the impact of their solution on their internal customers.

The team creates stories of success. They share them with others in the organization. Recognition drives support. People respond to stories. I hope you've responded to mine.

I wish you much success in your efforts to implement the Wheel of Sustainability. It has been my pleasure to deliver it to you.

LET'S CONNECT

I would love to hear your feedback and answer any questions you may have about the Wheel of Sustainability. Here's how to reach me:

- Email – atlawrence@pi-partners.com
- Phone – +1 (717) 947-5535
- Website – www.pi-partners.com
- LinkedIn Company Page – Process Improvement Partners
- LinkedIn Personal Page – Adam Lawrence
- YouTube Channel – Adam Lawrence

Summary of Services

All services are chartered to assure they meet the unique needs of your business:

Wheel of Sustainability Implementation – Take a deep dive into the Wheel and apply it to critical organizational work.

Site Assessment – This one-day process engages leadership and those who work in the process. During the assessment, we identify critical issues, improvement opportunities, and approaches to realize those improvements. At the end, we have a road map to deliver significant improvements and savings for the business.

Strategic Planning – Based on the principles of Lean and Value Stream Mapping. This effort uses a diverse, customer-focused team to deeply understand the current situation and the areas of opportunity. These opportunities are then scheduled to create a future that delivers breakthrough improvements in safety, productivity, customer service, and profitability.

Cultural Transformation – Leaders are coached, mentored, and participate in demonstrations of the drivers of cultural transformation. An ongoing, hands-on process to help the organization take full ownership for their transformation efforts.

Best Practice Facilitation – This one-day workshop is designed to help teams facilitate more productive meetings and events. Participants receive training through demonstrations, discussions, and hands-on activities. Ideally suited for groups of eight to twenty, it can be front-loaded into Kaizen event(s) for real-time application of skills.

Visual Management and Workforce Participation – What does it take to truly engage your work force and drive accountability for daily results? This workshop is designed to help build the plan and leadership actions to drive performance to higher levels and improve workforce engagement. This workshop can last between two and four days, depending on the scope of the effort.

Workplace Organization – A fun and fast-paced workshop, where teams realize significant productivity gains and safety risk reduction. Using Lean principles and 5S techniques, teams remove clutter, place things in their optimal locations, maintain resources in top condition, and implement the Wheel of Sustainability to sustain the improvements.

Changeover Reduction – Based on Lean principles and Single Minute Exchange of Die (SMED) techniques, teams remove waste and reduce effort in the changeover process. It's not unusual to create a safer, simpler, and more efficient method that reduces time required by 50 percent or more. The resulting improvements are locked in with the Wheel of Sustainability. This workshop lasts between $3\frac{1}{2}$ and $4\frac{1}{2}$ days.

Process Optimization – Using Lean principles and proven Standard Work methods, this workshop brings people together to determine the safest and most productive way to accomplish critical tasks. The team is guided to implement the Wheel of Sustainability to ensure everyone follows the improved process.

Training Within Industry – The proven method develops standard work and trains your organization in a way that will guarantee consistency and optimal performance. This intense workshop will help you develop and implement a strategy and tactics to benefit your organization and your customers.

Plant Reliability Improvement – Using Lean principles and proven Reliability techniques, this ongoing effort drives an organization to World Class Reliability utilizing Standard Work, Visual Management, Shop Floor Participation, Best Practice Maintenance, and Kaizen events. Assistance is provided until the organization takes ownership of the improvement efforts. Alternatively, this effort can be focused on a single underperforming process through a Kaizen event.

Breakthrough Creativity and Innovation – Using Lean principles and the Production Preparation Process (3P) approach, this workshop drives teams to uncover and implement breakthrough solutions to critical problems. Clients have said they accomplished more in this session than they had in the months leading up to it. Teams have developed and implemented new products, services, and processes during this $4\frac{1}{2}$ day Kaizen event.

Failure Prevention – Stop problems before they happen through the identification, prioritization, development, and implementation of preventative actions. Using Lean principles and Failure Modes and Effects Analysis (FMEA), organizations make significant reductions in the risk to people, processes, and their customers.

Cost Reduction Ideation, Prioritization, and Implementation – This three-day workshop challenges team members to come up with ideas to reduce costs in their business, without negatively impacting safety, quality, or customer experience. Once ideas have been generated, they're prioritized, organized, scoped out, and planned over a defined time horizon. Teams have regularly beaten savings targets, which can be in the millions of dollars.

Virtual Kaizen Events – Imagine bringing teams together from all over the world without the cost or hassle of travel. These sessions allow collaboration across time zones and in many cases are more productive than being together in the same location.

ACKNOWLEDGMENTS

It takes a village to write a book. I never knew what went into it, until I tried to do it myself. Many people helped and supported me along the way:

Peggy – She read every word many times and helped me simplify things so that others would understand what I was trying to say. She put up with me when I couldn't type another word and had to sit in our big, comfy, blue chair.

Tyler – He got me out of a bind many times, solving my computer problems

My Beta Readers – Tom Dardick, Norman Prentiss, Pennie Saum, and Elliott Weiss. If you like how the book flows, you can thank them. If not, you can blame me!

Tessa Shaffer – She was the first person to look at my writing and helped me turn it into something coherent. She calls herself a *"Book Doula"*. I didn't know what that meant until I met her.

Keith Bell – He created many of the graphics you see in the book.

My Kaizen Teams – I'm telling your stories. I hope I did them justice.

My Network – You have encouraged me many times to bring my Wheel to life. This is it, I hope I met your expectations.

ABOUT THE AUTHOR

Adam T. Lawrence
atlawrence@pi-partners.com
717.947.5535

Adam Lawrence is the Managing Partner of Process Improvement Partners, LLC. He has 30+ years of experience in process improvement activities, targeted at manufacturing and business processes. Having facilitated 300+ Kaizen events in multiple industries around the world, Adam aligns with leadership, engages teams, and creates sustainable results.

Adam has mastered the use of many different process improvement methodologies, allowing him to implement the best strategy for each organization's goals and objectives. He develops sessions that are fun, engaging, and laser-focused. Adam is 100 percent committed to ensuring the team has a winning result and a fantastic experience.

Married to his wonderful wife, Peggy, for over 29 years, they have one son (Tyler, his IT department). Adam grew up in the Washington, DC area and received his BS in Industrial Engineering from Virginia Tech. He earned Lean certifications from the University of Michigan.

Adam enjoys time with family and friends, loud music, traveling, the many great clients he has worked with (his extended family), and his many business adventures. *The Wheel of Sustainability* is his first book.

Printed in Great Britain
by Amazon

80931422R00169